STRANGER ANGELS

MORE TALES FROM THE

SELF-RIGHTEOUS HOUSEWIFE

BY JUDY ZIMMERMAN

Stranger Angels: More Tales From the Self Righteous House-Wife

Copyright © 2020 Judy Zimmerman / Jeff Ludwig / Paul Zimmerman

All rights reserved

Cover painting by Grace Ludwig

Cover photo by Atticus Ludwig

To self-righteous writers with a sense of humor all over the world.

CONTENTS

INTRODUCTION..7

PART 1: MOMS..11

Moms and Jason Bourne Skills, Skills, Season of Deceit, That Nearly Empty Nest, Deputy Mom, Dark Days of Winter, I Spy, Going Home, Buena Suerte Sra Serafa, Are You a Hoarder or a Pitcher?, I'm Fifty, Are You a Good Parent? I Remember You, Mindfully Neglectful, Your Someday Tattoo, Stay at Home Moms and Used Car Salesmen, 47,48,49 Oblivion, Prenatal, To Prom, Confirming I'm an Idiot

PART 2: KIDS..75

As the Nest Empties, Shopping for Big Brother, The Kissing Hand, The Kissing Hand: The Sequel, Hand Me Downs, To Kill a Mockingbird, To Kill a Mockingbird Part II: The Name, Teenage Boys: Delightful, 8th Grade Graduation, Prom, Upside-down Duck, Garbanzo Beans and Tablecloths

PART 3: SCHOOL..117

Disorienting, Moving out of the Dorm, Turnabout and the Photo Shoot, College Visits, Spare Keys, Caps and Gowns, Two Buttons Down, Two to Go, Don't Let the Door Hit You, Artists in Training, More About the School of The Art Institute, Limping Toward College, The ACTs, Au Revoir!, First Day of First Grade, Censorship, High School Has Changed in 30 Years

PART 4: ENTERTAINMENT..173

Aunt Delia & the Christmas Party, The Trump-inator, Glazed Ham, Summer Holidays, Country Strong, Report From Amsterdam, The Christmas Party, Halloween: Then and Now, What Would Tyra Do? The Arnold Story

PART 5: FRIENDS & FAMILY..205

The Zoo, Friends' Parents and Parents' Friends, It's All Relative, Pure Michigan, Texting 1-2-3, Michael Johnson, Crushes, Don't Ask Don't Tell, Just Hold a Towel Over the Window, I Wanna Hold Your Hand, Smile for the Camera

PART 6: RANDOM..239

My Dog Tells You About the Skunk, Beauty and Short Hair, Be Kind on Thursday, Free the Presidential Apostrophe, That Drawer and Band Polos, The Royal Wedding: Then and Now, iPad myPad, Facebook: Tidal Wave, FaceBook: Go Ahead and Try It, Paper or Plastic, Love Notes in Lunch Bags, A Love Story For Valentine's Day, I've Got Guys, More of What Passes for Conversation Around Here, Bathroom Remodel, Out of the Woods, The Summer of '03

PART 7: CANCER..295

Lilly Look Back, Casseroles Cure Cancer, Stranger Angels, That's Done: Period, Caringbridge and a Cooler, Okay, Enough of That, To Sleep Perchance to Dream, Drugs

AFTERWORD...321

FORWARD

The author with her mother Faye Zimmerman

L ife. Love. Family. Humor. And even cancer. My little sister Judy Zimmerman wrote about all of that in her blog *The Self Righteous Housewife*. She could find humor in just about anything writing from a northern suburb of Chicago right up to the point she died of leiomyosarcoma cancer in late 2013. She published a paperback collection of her blogs in 2012 called *Just Fake the Reading Log, Tales from the the Self-Righteous Housewife*. This volume collects dozens of others as she took on getting older, her three children Atticus, Grace and Lilly going off to school and her joyous adventures with husband Jeff Ludwig. And so much more. So here's the good and the bad divided up into seven nifty sections. Enjoy! She always did.

—Paul Zimmerman / May 2020

INTRODUCTION

Life is what happens when you are busy making plans. Isn't that the truth? When we are busy dreaming up all of our adventures, our good intentions, and conjuring up our life's story, it carries on mostly in a very unassuming way. Life is beautiful and tragic; joyful and sad. It reveals our shortcomings, our strengths and our vulnerabilities. It summons up our courage from time to time and it shines an unflattering bright light on all of our fears. The wisdom of that one beautiful line was not lost on my wife, the author of this book – her second collection of stories.

Speaking of the author. Her stories give you a little glimpse into her style, her temperament, and her soberingly authentic view of the world. Her work stands on its own, so I'll avoid the temptation of telling you how smart, gifted, creative and funny Judy was. See what I did there? Instead, I'll try to bring to life why I and so many others were drawn to her. And how falling in love, being in love and loving her big and hard as she asked, was so easy during our 32 years together. Of course, once and a while it was not – but if you've been married for anytime at all, you understand that. Loving Judy was simple except on those occasions when it was not - when it required one to pursue a deeper understanding of the insane world up close that she seemed to grasp so effortlessly and was impatient with those of us (me) who could not.

Judy had a very sharp edge and you did not want to find yourself on the cutting end of it. Judy's loyalty and commitment to (fill in the blank) was unwavering and unconditional. Judy's confidence in her decisions was intimidating, inspiring and comforting. She never second guessed, she never looked back and she never apologized for not being like- minded. Against the advice of all her mom friends, she took Lilly out of pre-school because of the anxiety it caused her to be apart from her mom that first year after her battle with cancer. Moms whispered and Judy smiled with Lilly in tow anxious to share her newest political outrage or community gossip.

Red was her favorite color – duh. She greeted me at the Cherry Capital airport on New Year's Eve many years in a sparkling gown and a Manhattan. She had undergraduate degrees in Economics and Spanish and an MBA in International Marketing. She was on her way to becoming the CEO of a global company until she in her own words, "could not do anything more important than raise children to be kind, caring, and helpful in the world". Her drink of choice – Cosmo.

She called the kids out of school one beautiful spring day telling the school administrator they all had Cubs fever and then she took them to the game. She loved musicals – her favorite, West Side Story. She loved Abba which I never understood. She put her foot in her mouth often; the unfortunate consequence of always having an opinion and no ability to suffer fools, ignorance and most of all intolerance. Among her many heroes – Morris Dees and Atticus Finch. She had as many little black dresses in her closet as she did ball gowns which were many. With her first bonus as a young marketing executive with World Book Encyclopedia, she treated herself to a leather miniskirt; me to a box of cigars; and then she gave the rest to the Southern Poverty Law Center. She could go from crow to a headstand.

A couple of paragraphs don't get close to who she was, but if you were not blessed to know her, maybe you get some sense for what all the fuss is about.

Judy's love of life was her superpower. She filled me and our children with so much love during her short 53 years – I think she knew all along that it had to be enough to sustain us for as long as we are to be without her. Her final word of advice to us all was to love as big and as hard as we can. That makes me smile.

I write this in honor of my wife and her superpower – her ability to live and love big, and her ability to show us all how to do the same. I miss her. Our incredibly kind, caring, and helpful children are all I need to fulfill me when I am lonely for her. Also, her stories make me laugh. Enjoy.

—Jeffrey Ludwig / February 2020

PART 01: MOMS

MOMS AND JASON BOURNE SKILLS

Husband Jeff LOVES Matt Damon. Well, who doesn't love Matt Damon? But he has a total man-crush on him and and admires Matt's considerable on-screen skills at evading the bad guys when he is playing Jason Bourne.

(Real quick, in case you do not know, Jason Bourne is like James Bond only he has amnesia so he does not even KNOW who the bad guy is at any given moment!)

Anyhoo, Jeff decided while we were on vacation, that he was going to scope out new hotel rooms and lobbies and coffee shops as if HE were Jason Bourne. Then he shared this fun activity with us.

Which is why the five of us were standing in the open foyer of our hotel in Half Moon Bay in Northern California, a few weeks ago, as Jeff explained how he would escape from the second-floor atrium if he were Jason Bourne and had to evade a bad-guy. This plan involved hurdtling over the balcony, bouncing off the ottoman below, and parkouring (aka freerunning) against the elevator before shooting out the back exit.

The next morning, when Jeff and I had our coffee and pastry at a little shop around the corner, we watched as a young mom with two young children came in the store, holding the kids' hands carefully, looking over her sunglasses, and then scanning the room at the same time.

"Have you ever noticed," Jeff said, nodding his head in her direction, "how moms with little kids come into a restaurant or store and sort of scope it out like she's doing? It's, well, it's kind of like..."

"Like Jason Bourne?" I finished. Oh yeah, I have noticed that before because: That's. What. Good. Moms. Do.

We watched her order, pay, get the necessary napkins and stirrers, dispense the food, and calmly exit through the side door with no fuss. She was quiet, not one of those loud, self-narrarating, talking in the third-person moms (what is up with that anyway?). In short, she was as cool as, well as an international spy on a special ops mission.

Afterwards, I spent much of the day thinking of *all the ways* she was like an international spy and I came up with this list of what Jason Bourne and effective moms have in common when going out to eat or shop. If you think of more, let me know.

1. You must be willing to abort the mission at ANY time: That's right. You may be Jason Bourne or a young mom but the number one rule of survival is that if something, anything goes amiss, *you have to be willing to leave* before the mission is accomplished.

It does not matter if you just traveled to Moscow in a van from Bucharest with that spy girl you met and have not eaten since Slovenia or you just traveled fifteen minutes from home in the mini-van after waiting almost 24 hours for that first sip of your perfect latte—if you spot a guy in the corner with a watch-cap pulled over his eye who looks like former KGB or if one of your kids is about to have a melt-down because you did not time breakfast just right—TOO BAD for you.

CODE RED CODE RED LEAVE THE PREMISES LEAVE NOW, I REPEAT LEAVE NOW

For Jason, it is a matter of life and death. For the young mother it is a little more important.

Because when you are on a mission out in the real world with kids you are not just trying to get to the store and get something and avoid being embarrassed but you are trying to *parent* on top of it all. Jason just has to stay alive.

My friend Mary W.B. taught me this lesson early on and it proved invaluable. She made her point by telling a story of an incident that had happened to her (this was many years ago: her kids are in college now).

She had schemed for weeks to get out of the house with her tots and meet another mom and her kids for lunch at Applebees. As soon as they got there, one of her kids starting having a fit about something he wanted on the menu.

Mary warned him once to knock it off or they would leave. He did not. He gambled that his mom was hungry enough and wanted to visit with her friend enough that she'd cave in and he'd get what he wanted.

Well, he picked the wrong mom. She DID want to visit with her friend. And she WAS hungry, but when he acted up again, she calmly put money on the table to cover the drinks, apologized to her friend, scooped up the kids and left. Everyone got peanut butter and jelly for lunch at home that day.

And that never happened to her again.

Mary told that story, then looked around and said, "Remember, you have to be willing to leave at any time, otherwise *they* have the upper hand." She looked like she knew what she was talking about and I took note. And she's right, if you employ this tactic you will permanently disarm your terrorist. If you give in even once, you've put the weapon back in his hand.

Not even Jason Bourne has that kind of power.

2. Know where the bathroom is: Moms need to know where the bathrooms are for obvious reasons. But it isn't enough to know where it is—you also need to know if all the children with you will fit in the bathroom (if the kids are all very young) and if you do need to use the opposite sex bathroom (if the kids are a bit older but not old enough to go alone) how that is going to go down.

Mom also needs to be able to go the bathroom herself while balancing any non-walking children on her lap and corralling the other kids in the stall, and she needs to figure out what can be used as a changing table if there isn't one available.

Jason Bourne needs to know where the bathroom is because the tiny window in that room is ALWAYS the ONLY way Jason will escape if the other exits are blocked.

It's possible Jason Bourne has the easier job here.

3. Spot the two or three areas of potential danger: While Jason Bourne is figuring out if there is an assassin behind the potted plant or a barista with poison, mom has her own issues to deal with. Is one of the kids what we call a toucher? The kid who has to touch everything? A clumsy toucher? Worse combo ever....quickly, she must get between her and that display of coffee mugs. Is one a curious dissembler—he likes to take things apart for fun? She must immediately get between him and the espresso machines for sale.

Young mom also knows to head all children off in front of the treat case by "selling" what they CAN have never what they CAN'T "Here's a nice muffin or fruit plate, which do you prefer?" as she keeps her gaze away from the cake-pop.

Meanwhile, Jason has figured out it's safe to go ahead and order an espresso. Or not.

4. Spot the two or three things that will serve as a distraction if needed:
The flip side of distracting a small child (or the leader of a terrorist cell) from trouble is to find something constructive to amuse them with first.

This is why Jason Bourne always leads with a charm defense by chatting up or flirting with the spy before going for a throat punch. Much easier.

The young mom sees quickly that the stir sticks make an awesome game of pickup sticks. Drinking little cups of creamer is a dream come true for most toddlers. And those toys for sale that the coffee shop manager has diabolically put on the bottom shelf at kid level—well you can just explain they are "not for sale because they live in the store and are to visit with".

Distraction is great and here young mom does have an easier job than Jason Bourne because secret spies are seldom distracted by the flip-side of a paper placemat and a pile of crayons.

These are just some of the things that come to mind. There is probably a whole essay to be written on how Jason Bourne and young mothers keep enough clothing on hand at all times to completely change a disguise or a toddler's outfit after a total pull-up blow out.

My young mom days are long gone but I admire watching the new recruits as they learn and bring their own experience to the job.

So if you're new to the mom as black ops agent, please know I am like "M" (sorry, that is a James Bond reference but you get the idea) and I am watching and admiring your mad secret spy skills.

SEASON OF DECEIT

It's May, I have a senior in high school, and EVERYTHING happens this month. Concerts, end-of-year banquets, the award ceremony, Prom, Senior Ditch Day, Graduation, and for our family— —both girls' birthdays.

For me, my main job in all of this, appears to be lying.

First, the girls asked me if they could skip PE (first period for both of them) to go out to breakfast on Lilly's birthday. Now here I should mention, (which is code for I will try to explain my bad behavior) this is the ONLY year the girls have been in the same school. They are very, very close, and they are not looking forward to their impending separation.

So I decided sure, why not. They can miss PE and make a memory for a lifetime.

The only problem was I had to "call them out" by calling the school to excuse their late arrival.

Now I hate to lie outright so I just said the girls had "a family commitment" which is kind of true.

A few days later, Grace wanted to get called out early to get ready for prom. Now here I should mention, prom is on a Friday night. So really, how can a girl get ready if she waits until after school to start that process (never mind that the entire girls' soccer team managed to win regionals, get their trophy and still make it to prom looking ravishing—the rest of the class needed hours to get ready).

Since I hate to lie outright, this time I said, "Grace has to leave early. She has a doctor's appointment to get her hair done for prom."

Next up, you guessed it, Senior Ditch Day. Now here I should mention, even I, the biggest goody-two-shoes in the world partook in Senior Ditch Day (but I think we called it Senior Skip Day). Never mind, I see no harm in this either. The school year is SO done by now for the Seniors it is time to put a fork in it. She would miss nothing, she has all A's, so I agreed.

And since I hate to lie outright, I called the attendance office and said "Grace can't come to school today because she has to see the doctor about a bad case of Senioritis.

I am relieved to say that I do not have to lie anymore to the school. This year.

But tomorrow morning I have to come up with a lie because I am supposed to leave the house before Grace to attend the Awards Ceremony and for some reason, the school asks that we keep this a secret from the kids. I

NEVER leave the house before the girls so—yes—I have to come up with a lie to tell Grace about why I'm leaving the house so early.

I'm thinking of telling Grace I have to go to the doctor to be seen for a bad case of sociopathic lying.

At least that would be partly true.

I hope you are enjoying the Merry Month of May and that you haven't had to lie too much.

THAT NEARLY EMPTY NEST

Text from my neighbor: Just watching "The Middle"
Is it us?

It was funny to get that text last night because I happened to be watching "The Middle" at the same time and it wasn't even on right then: both of us were watching it a day late on our DVR.

I also happened to be thinking the same thing.

For those of you who don't watch the show, it is a family sit-com starring Patricia Heaton as a mom in "The Middle" meaning the mid-west but it could also mean the middle years. It is uncannily accurate in the portrayal of a 50 ish mom.

In this episode, her character, Frankie, was trying to get a job and the employers kept asking her "So who IS Frankie?" which had set off an identity crisis. After 19 years of parenting three kids she was not so sure anymore. (Parenting three kids for 19 years. Why does that sound familiar?)

My neighbor is a true empty-nester—her singlet is a junior in college. I still have the girls at home—but not for long. Now that everyone is in high-school and beyond...well I haven't moved into the empty nest but I certainly need to start shopping for one.

This is a way harder time than other moms let on. Sometimes you catch a glimpse of honesty on the topic. As I re-read (for at least the tenth time) A Gift from the Sea, by Anne Morrow Lindbergh while on vacation last month, I came upon this paragraph I had not recalled, in an epilogue she had added some 20 years after first writing the essay book on parenting and marriage:

*"When I wrote **Gift from the Sea**, I was still in the stage of life I called "the oyster bed," symbol of a spreading family and growing children. The oyster bed, as the tide of life ebbed and the children went away to school, college, marriage or careers, was left high and dry. A most uncomfortable stage followed not sufficiently anticipated and barely hinted at in my book. In bleak honesty it can only be called "the abandoned shell." Plenty of solitude, and sudden panic at how to fill it, characterize this period. With me, it was not a question of simply filling up the space or time. I had many activities and even a well-established vocation to pursue. But when a mother is left, the lone hub of a wheel, with no other lives revolving about her, she faces a total re-orientation. It takes time to re-find the center of gravity."*

Many of you have careers outside the home so perhaps do not feel quite so lost or lost at all. For those of us fortunate enough to make the choice to be stay-at-home moms, well, I feel like the reverse of that t-shirt that said "Oops, I forgot to have babies"! Mine could say, "Oops, I forgot to go back to work".

So now what? For many of us, age, health concerns, and ailing parents, not to mention a job market that is not exactly looking for a woman who hasn't worked in 20 years, keeps us from readily re-entering that world.

Many will overcome those obstacles; many already have.

I don't know what's next. Like Frankie Heck, I don't know quite how to answer that question, "So who IS Judy."

But at least I know I am not doing it alone. Because if my neighbor feels that way, and the writers of "The Middle" know it, and Anne Morrow Lindbergh in 1975 wrote about it....it's pretty universal.

Best wishes to us all as we seek to "re-find the center of gravity."

DEPUTY MOM

When you become a mom you are instantly deputized by the powers of the universe to do mom things like help children who have toppled off bicycles or approach a child who is obviously lost. In the past you may have thought, "I wonder if I should try to help?" or when you were much younger you really did not even notice a kid who fell off a bike, but now you know viscerally that you must help. And not only that you must help but that you have all the authority needed to take charge because—you are a mom.

The magic powers that make you a Deputy Mom are not the same powers that turn you into Super Mom. Super Mom powers are those that enable you, who are so squeamish you literally had to put your head down between your legs or you would have passed out when a friend told you about a particularly gory episode with a broken glass, to look your toddler in the eye while holding a washcloth to a cut on his chin that reveals bone, and say calmly, "We may have to go to the ER for this one."

Usually you realize you possess this power the first time you encounter a large spider near your new baby. Though you have spent your entire life dealing with spiders by shrieking for help from the nearest person in the house and/or closing the door and simply not going in the room where the spider is for a few days, you realize at that moment that you and only you must kill the spider. And then you do it—because you are Super Mom.

Super Mom powers and Deputy Mom powers come from the same place: a very clear realization that if you don't take care of this no one will. But Super Mom powers are used to protect your own child from danger where as Deputy Mom powers are used to help make this world a better place in general.

With Deputy Mom powers you have the right, nay the obligation, to help or correct all endangered or misguided children as needed. You may find yourself calling out to a teen on a skateboard, "Hey, where's your helmet?" or to a tween, "Watch your language I've got toddlers here!" (I must mention here that I live in a place where the children are all incredibly polite and usually answer with a wave and a "Sorry" instead of an "Up yours old lady" like they would have when I was growing up.)

There is only one very important rule when you invoke your Deputy Mom authority and that is you must never, never, never use the power if the parent of the errant or imperiled child is present. That is poor form. But feel free to tell the potty-mouth in the carpool, "Oh dear no, Justin, we do not say Mother Fucker in this van."

Fathers are also deputized but they seldom use their authority to call kids out on safety violations. For one thing, safety violations often go undetected by them or even admired as an act of boyhood derring-do as in , "Look that kid is getting towed on his skate board by his brother driving that SUV! That looks so fun!" So don't count on them to get the neighborhood hoodlum to wear sneakers instead of flip-flops when he mows the lawn but they should feel moved to correct rude or unkind behavior.

Once when we were leaving the movies a teen called out to a girl he knew. When she turned to smile at him he MOOED at her! Jeff grabbed the kid by the shoulder, "Did you just moo at that girl?" he asked in a tone that clearly conveyed he did not find that acceptable. The kid tried to deny it but Jeff would have none of it, "Yes you did. I saw the whole thing. That is the most unkind thing I've ever seen anyone do and if I ever see you do it again you will be very, very sorry." Now I have known Jeff for nearly 30 years and I can tell you, though is he a champion of the underdog, he never did stuff like that before he had kids.

So if you are a new mom (Leslie) I dedicate this blog to you and I officially deputize you and your spouse (Chris) as keepers of civilization.

MOMMY WARS? NO SUCH THING

So I have been a stay-at-home mom for 18 years now and every few years some numb-skull says something to unintentionally insult stay-at-home moms and the press just picks it up and RACES away with it turning it into cover stories and blog fodder and yaddah yaddah yaddah.

And each time I have to sort of mull it over and wonder how I feel about this supposed "war" in which I am in.

This most recent skirmish got me thinking again and I have come to several conclusions that I thought I might share for those of you who are in this "battle" or merely observing it from afar.

Here's what I have learned in 18 years of "fighting".

There is no mommy-war.

It's completely made up by the press for something to talk about and maybe a handful of mommies who really are conflicted about their own choice.

For the rest of us, it does not exist. In 18 years I have literally never heard a stay-at-home mom bash a working mom for that decision. Never.

Sometimes I hear a stay-at-home comment that it looks like it would be awfully hard to work full-time but that is about it. When I worked, I never heard a working mom disparage a stay-at-home. Sometimes I heard a working-mom say staying at home looked boring but that was about it.

Let me organize my thoughts even more with a few bullet-points—because I love bullet-points.

1. The issue of stay-at-home vs. working is not an economic issue (though that topic gets muddled into the debate frequently)—what I mean is if you are talking about the value of a woman staying home raising kids versus the value of her working outside the home while raising kids you are by definition taking the *need* to work out of the equation.

No this is not nice for women who have to work—they have no choice—but it is not the issue at hand—if you have to work you have to work there is no debate about your decision to do so.

It is like trying to have a conversation about anorexia and having someone point out that there are starving people in the world. Yes, there certainly are and that fact does put the issue in perspective—but it does not address the issue at hand.

2. Here, where there are boots on the ground, there is not much animosity between these two groups (despite all media hype to the contrary including TV and movies): Because our best friends, sisters, and neighbors (or even

we have been working moms), we are not really into hating on each other. I seldom hear these terms even come up.

As for the working moms bashing on us...well the worst thing I read in the last go-around was that sometimes we are called "LuLuLemon Moms" because we wear yoga clothes all day. Really? This is the meanest thing you can say about us? Yes, it's true we do wear our yoga clothes but you wear nice work suits! So na-na-na-na-boo-boo!

3. Everyone hates their job and envies someone else's job sometimes — this does not constitute a war: My husband, a successful corner-office-clawed-his-way-to-the-top business guy sometimes (okay a lot of time) wishes he played lead guitar in a rock band. But he does not go around bashing all men who chose to pursue a music career. He might envy them, but he doesn't try to tell them they should "get a day job". We stay-at-home/working moms are no different. Sometimes we regret what we chose, usually we are happy, we try not to be envious.

4. Bottom line is we all do what we can and what we have to do to make the best life for family and ourselves. If you find yourself getting very worked up over this topic, perhaps it is yourself you are struggling with. As has been suggested before by many wiser than I, it might just be that the mommy-war is an internal struggle.

As for the rest of us, we can always meet up at the end of a work day (wherever that may take place) and discuss our common lives (being mommies) over a glass of wine.

That doesn't look like a war to me.

DARK DAYS OF WINTER

A while back Lilly was complaining that I repeat myself a lot. I do. I repeat myself a lot. So I said, "Look, tell me the top three things I repeat the most and I'll try not to say them too much."

She cocked her head and thought a minute. "Make me a Cosmo. I'm going to take a nap. Can't you get a ride?"

In my defense, I never say, "Make me a Cosmo," to the kids. Not one of my kids can handle a martini shaker properly. No, I say that to Jeff. Or more accurately, I say "Cosmo me." But I do announce I'm taking a nap a lot and for sure I ask, "Can't you get a ride?"

That's because here in Glenview, the kids need a ride ALL THE FLIPPING TIME and even though they are all going to the same three places—The Glen (our shopping area); the High School; or back to our neighborhood—and even though they all have cell phones with the number programmed in of every kid they have met since pre-school, not one of them, no not one single one will use said cell phone to text a friend and say, "Hey, can I catch a ride with you?"

Which is why all of us moms are driving the same two miles to and from and saying "Can't you get a ride?" and waving to each other. Of course, we're almost as bad because at nearly every cocktail party and school event, we talk about the absurdity and wastefulness of this practice and say, "Call me if you need me to get the kids," but we never really do it and I don't know why except no one wants to be the mom of the kid who is constantly bumming rides.

This little scenario gets worse this time of year because it gets dark at 4:30. And it turns out that even though electricity has been around a long time and we all stay up much past 4:30 in the winter, our bodies don't really like it. We don't care to go out in the freezing cold and wipe large amounts of snow off our cars and drive around on roads like ice-rinks in the wintry darkness. We have no problem in the summer when it is light until 9:30 dropping kids and picking kids up but this time of year we rather hate this part of the job.

Recently I learned that a lot of my mom friends hate the winter for just this reason. I learned I am not the only one who counts the trips off in her head during the winter, "One trip to middle school, one round trip to piano, then one last trip to the high school," and then when that last trip is done, after counting heads and making sure all the kids are home, I lock the door so none will escape and race upstairs to throw my pajamas on.

So today, if you are wishing it were summer or light out or that your children weren't quite so active as you shuttle them around, please know you aren't the only one that feels that way this time of year. And also know that tonight, if all goes well, I'll be in my pajamas by around 6:30.

I SPY

I was recently with some mom-friends when one of them mentioned her adolescent son was starting to get text messages from girls. "Oh, it was harmless though. I went back later and read them all and it was just silly talk."

This casual admission of invading her son's privacy made me, umm, queasy. I know, I know, everyone does this. Now that we can peek into our children's lives via electronic media it's easy to do but I'm not sure that makes it right.

I grew up in a house where personal privacy was highly regarded. I could have left my diary (had I kept one) open on my bed-stand and my mother would have walked by and gently closed it without looking. I extend the same courtesy to my own children.

I have wrestled with this thing since I see so many of my peers *peering* and see that some even consider cyber-spying to be good parenting. I'm not so sure.

So in an effort to help myself understand this a little better, I offer the following points of consideration:

1. **First, ask yourself why you are spying.** Do you have some reason to be generally concerned for your child's safety (drugs, abusive relationship, bullying) or are you simply spying because you can—or because it is entertaining or because it makes you feel like you have a little control as they grow up and more out of your control. That's not nice. Would you like your spouse or your children to hack into your email just for fun or just to see what you are up to? Probably not.

2. **Try to think of the cyber-communication in terms of something you already understand and have established boundaries for**—for example, texting is a little like a phone call—it's direct communication from one person to another, not intended for anyone else to see/hear. Would you ever pick up the receiver in the other room and listen in? E-mail is similar and is like a letter—would you ever open your child's mail? I hope not as that is a federal offense.

3. **If you do decide to spy, alert your kids first.** It's only fair to give your kids a head's up. Simply declare that going forward you reserve the right to peek in on their Facebook account (or whatever) from time to time. Facebook is a little more like a public space and therefore it is not as invasive as spying on emails or texts. It is said Facebook is like the mall—although that said, would you go to the mall and follow your kid around eavesdropping on his conversations?

So there you have it. Some food for thought as we navigate these new high-tech media-crazy times. To quote The Onion, "Now the only thing keeping you from spying on your kid is having a life of your own!"

GOING HOME

Though Jeff and I moved to the Chicago area 24 years ago, we still sometimes say "going home" when talking about going back to Michigan for family events or visits. Last weekend I went home for my sister's retirement party. I don't get back there very often anymore.

Before kids we went home every few months. When the kids were very little we still tried to get there for major holidays and events but not so much anymore.I don't like this but what can you do? When you move away four hours (now up to six hours thanks to ever-increasing and unavoidable Chicago traffic) and when you go from two of you to five of you (and two of them are teenagers with lives of their own) you aren't as mobile as you'd like to be.

This does not make the people back home happy. My mother gamely tells me about every baby shower, dance recital, and pig roast that she thinks I should attend involving any of my dozens of cousins (some of them are HER second cousins, I don't even know what that makes them to me, twice removed or something) but for the most part we just can't pull it off which is why we're down to weddings, funerals, reunions, and retirements (for parents/grandparents/siblings/nieces & nephews only).

Those who have not moved away from home and indeed some who have not moved out of the zip code they were raised in, are not very understanding or sympathetic of those of us who have. In fact, I have come to realize there are a lot of unwritten rules about an arrangement like this. I know from talking to other friends who have "moved away" that these rules are pretty universal. Here are some of the unwritten rules I've learned in 24 years of living away from "back home".

1) If you are the one who moved away, you are the one who has to come visit. It does not work the other way around. Yes, this defies logic and even common sense but still the grandmas and the aunties like to say "Gosh, it's been a long time since you came to visit" even though most of them have never been to your home or have been only once a long, long time ago.

2) No matter how long it has been since you moved away; no matter how far away you now live; no matter how busy you are; no matter how many kids of your own you have; no matter how much traffic you must battle—you are still expected to attend major events. I don't know if this applies to people when they get to a certain level of busy-ness or have so clearly made a new life for themselves far away. Maybe Oprah's cousins still ask if she will be attending the annual Thanksgiving dinner. Perhaps George Clooney's sister expects him to attend her daughter's ballet recital. I don't know but I know in my family and in most families, this stuff is still expected.

3) It is the right, nay the duty, of those who have chosen to stay in the childhood town to make fun of those who moved to "the big city." Though you would not make fun of the podunk town you have escaped, they feel free to tell you that they would NEVER live in the city you have chosen. The traffic is awful, there are too many people, the housing is outrageous, and the last time they visited they had to pay $6.00 for a Coors Light!

4) It's best to sneak into town and out of town without telling too many people. No matter how many of the family and friends you want to visit you will never be able to see them all so you will have to resort to sneaking in to town. My sister now does this to me since two of her three kids live about 20 minutes from me. The fact is by the time you make the long drive and have a nice visit with whomever you've come to see you have NO energy or desire to try to cram in one more visit. I'm okay with that since I've had to do it for about 24 years now. And finally, the most important rule of all:

5) Regardless of how long you've been away, and how much you love where you live it's nice to know that when you go back home, you are always welcome. Because that's what home is all about.If I've missed any more rules (Jennifer K. I'm thinking of you by the way) please let me know.

BUENA SUERTE SRA SERAFA

My former high school Spanish teacher, Ms. Serafa is retiring this month and I wanted to send her a photo of the fantastic trip to Spain she took us on in the summer of '77. So I dusted off my photo album and found this picture. Atticus (16)looked at it with disbelief. "Is that girl holding a cigarette?" he asked—yes, I explained, students used to smoke in front of their teachers if they were over 16. , "And what's in all those cups?" Beer and wine silly! We were in Spain for crying out loud!

Sometimes when I regale my kids with a story of my own teen years Atticus will sigh and say, "You guys had so much fun." Usually this is in reference to something stupid and reckless we did which is now prohibited (which would be pretty much everything)—such as doing donuts in the school parking lot on a snowy day or cruisin' down Main Street with six or seven girls in the car, the radio turned up, and one of us hanging on to a coat hanger because the car antennae had long since fallen off. Current laws forbid driving in a car with more than one non-related teenager until you are 18. The law is perfectly sensible but not much fun.

This picture is just photographic evidence of a time long gone when kids were allowed to get in trouble some times and teachers and parents did not bail their asses out if they did. At our last reunion a friend reminded me of a band trip they had taken to Jamaica in the late 70's. On the way back through customs, one of the drug dogs sniffed out the pot the drummer had (surprise) and the police pulled him aside. When it came time to board the plane the police were still working the idiot over. One of the chaperones said to Willie, our band director, "Hey what are we going to do about him?" and Willie said, "F*** him. We're going home." And they did. No one got sued. I don't think anyone was even annoyed with Willie for leaving the chucklehead there. In fact, I think his parents let him sit in a Jamaican jail a day or two before coming to get him.

Yes, kids. These things really did happen once upon a time in America. Kids got in trouble and their parents made them pay the consequences without the help of attorneys and phone calls made to authorities (well, unless you were a Kennedy).

It was indeed a different time and I thank Ms. Serafa and her husband Pete who were only in their mid-20s when they took us all to Europe and allowed us to have fun and even if it meant we might get into trouble. I thank them for turning a blind eye to some of our behavior and thank Pete for pretending to believe us when we missed curfew and said it was because we had not set our watches to local time (three weeks into the trip). It was a great trip and I know it changed my life, opening up a world I did not know existed and showing a sheltered girl from the suburbs everything from the running of the bulls in Pamplona to the majesty of the Alhambra in Granada to the late night discos of Madrid.

Now, thanks to overprotective parents and aggressive law suits most teachers don't take these trips. Those who do go have to impose such restrictions on the kids and themselves that they pretty much take all the fun out of travel (a teacher friend recently chaperoned a trip to Ireland. No one, not even the adults when they were alone, had a beer. Not one beer on a trip to Ireland. I weep for humanity.)

So today I salute Ms. Serafa as she moves on from her 35 years of teaching. I thank her of course for her countless hours of fantastic classroom teaching. And I thank her and Pete for showing Europe to me and so many others for the first time. I wish them well as they move on to the next adventure in their lives and I hope they can have a fraction of the fun we all did that summer.

And to Atticus I say, you will have plenty of your own fun and you will be ultimately safer than we were.

But you're right, sometimes, we did have more fun.

ARE YOU A HOARDER OR A PITCHER?

We had a dumpster in the driveway a few weeks back. Nothing gets the neighbors talking like a dumpster in the driveway and I don't blame them. You see a dumpster and you know something big is going on—anything from a new bathroom all the way up to a complete house demolition.

So when my neighbors inquired about it I had fun giving them the truth—no project, *just throwing some stuff away*.

People reacted to this intel in two distinct ways—they either 1) became completely puzzled as to how someone could fill a dumpster of everyday household items or 2) were instantly smitten with the idea and wanted to know how to order one. The difference is based on whether the listener was a hoarder or a pitcher. I am obviously a pitcher. I am an extreme pitcher. If you set it down and don't use it for a few days I am likely to throw it out. Stuff does not make me feel good or comforted. It makes me feel smothered and claustrophobic.

As with all big house projects I didn't just wake up one day and say "I think I'll order a dumpster." No, it started with a small and simple sentence when Wine Friend 1 mentioned that she'd heard second refrigerators use a lot of electricity and we should unplug them. This is particularly relevant around here because just about everyone has a second refrigerator left over from a remodel (done back in the go-go mid-2000s) when we all put it in the garage or basement and filled it with extra beer. Then our kids became teenagers and we all emptied our refrigerators.

I went home and checked what was in my second fridge and found two boxes of very old Girl Scout cookies, a dish of pudding circa 2007, and crickets for Lilly's pet frog. I pitched it all (except the crickets) and unplugged the fridge.

But this story goes on in *If You Give a Mouse a Cookie* fashion because the very next day I was driving along when I heard an ad on the radio from ComEd telling me if I unplugged my second fridge they would come and haul it away AND pay me $25. The only caveat was they needed easy access to it. Which was a problem because it was in the basement in the former laundry room buried under seven years of crap and after careful consideration I decided there was really too much junk to just move it around into different piles. What I needed was to get rid of it all. What I needed was a dumpster. But, I wondered, how does *that* work?

The very next day I had my final Church Lady breakfast of the year and I threw the question out to the crowd. They are a very resourceful group of women and I knew if anyone would know, they would know. They did. Call our garbage service and they will bring you any size dumpster you want then pick it up when you want (for a price of course).

And that's why there was a dumpster in our driveway a couple weeks ago. First I cleared out the basement, then Jeff moved on to the shed, and finally he finished up with that attic above the garage. He was skeptical at first that we could fill a dumpster but we filled that puppy to the brim.

I share this with you all so that if you are a pitcher you may know how simple it is to achieve pitching nirvana. If you live with a hoarder, I am sorry as I know you could never pull this off and I know your opposing views on stuff cause domestic strife.
As for me, I'm just happy as a clam, light as a feather, and pleased as punch to be 6 square yards of junk lighter.

Oh yeah, and I got rid of the second fridge too. Thanks ComEd!

I'M FIFTY

So today I turn fifty and I thought I ought to say something about this momentous occasion. I don't have any particular wisdom to impart so I'll just share some random thoughts about the whole thing. To all my peers, NHS class of '78, this one's for you:

- First of all I have to say that fifty really is old. You can no longer put a good spin on it and saying "Fifty is the new forty" does not make it so. No matter how you slice it you are well into middle age and on your way to old age. But I don't find this dismaying—instead I find it liberating. We are grownups and we can stop running so fast and let those younger people carry some of the weight. At last we have arrived.

-At fifty you should stop trying to suck your stomach in. As a friend once said, "The other day I noticed the cat was sitting on my lap. Then I remembered I don't have a cat." The point is, by 50 everyone has a cat sitting on his or her lap. Stop trying to fight it. Enjoy your cat. Exhale.

-We are happier: new studies out just this week declare it so. Happiness peaks at 18, declines rapidly as the real world throws its crap at us and doesn't pick up again until we are 50. So if you feel as good as you did your senior year in high school, you are probably 50 or older. Life IS good.

-People who fight too hard against aging look foolish. Madonna and Melanie Griffith come to mind. Yes they might be thinner or tauter but they are also kind of freaky. They do not look better. So do not try to be like them. As my friend Christie Mellor says in the title of her book, "You Look Fine, Really". Most people would rather look at Meryl Streep than Madonna. Embrace your inner Meryl Streep.

-And finally, when you have an older sister, mother, and grandmother still alive and all quite active, how old can you really feel? Yes, when my sister got her first AARP card (8 years ago) she said it made her feel old. Then my mom pointed out that when your first child gets her AARP card you feel old. Then my grandma chimed in saying that when your first grandchild gets her AARP card you feel really old. So how old can I feel? We have many more years ahead and miles to go before we sleep. Just ask my grandma.

Happy birthday to the class of '78. Happy birthday to us all.

ARE YOU A GOOD PARENT?

These are the days of self-doubt and reflection for me and my peers. Many of us are coming up on 50 and our kids are about to launch into the real world. With this collision of events you could not be human without having doubts about where you are in life and whether or not you've done a good job with the kids.

I just spent time with a friend who expressed doubts about her parenting. This was shocking since she has—by anyone's assessment—some of the most talented and nicest children I know. But still she wonders if she's done enough and worries that mistakes have been made. This is proof I suppose that only a bad parent would never question the job he or she has done. The good ones take a look at it frequently and readjust as needed.

But how **are** we supposed to know if were doing a good job? Too many parents look to the easy assessments—grades, advanced/honors classes, elite college acceptance, awards, athletic accomplishments, invitations to dances. Yes all of these achievements (or lack of them) are easy to quantify but that doesn't make them valid assessors. We know they tell a very incomplete story. We know the super star athlete who is so stressed by the pressure he commits suicide or the over-achiever with the big smile who has a secret eating disorder. We also know these superficial measures of success do not predict future achievements or happiness. We've seen it all by now, the valedictorian who didn't do much; the homecoming queen thrice divorced;

the captain of the football team who never surpassed the glory of his senior year. So how DO we know if we've been doing a good job?

My friend Christie Mellor has a list of how to measure success that I like very much in her new book "You Look Fine, Really" which deals with the self-doubt women in their 40's and 50's have that leads them to do silly things like get plastic surgery or inject their wrinkles with botulism. She also talks about the bigger self-doubts like wondering what on earth we've done with our life—doubts that make us wonder if we are successful. Then she lists a wonderfully insightful and reassuring check-list for us all. She suggests we:

"...take a cold, hard look at what the heck you have been doing for the last forty or fifty years. Have you been learning new stuff? Have you become friends with some good people? Do your friends love you and do you love them? Do you laugh on a regular basis? Are you excited about what's coming next? Then you're a very, very successful person."

I thought of this list today after I talked to my friend and inspired by Christie I have a similar list—this one to determine if you have been a successful parent:

Take a good long look at your child. Is he kind? Is he respectful of you, teachers, grandparents, and his siblings? Does he help when he sees someone in need? Is he very good at something (it does not matter what —just one thing that is "his thing")? Does he know how to work hard to

achieve a goal? Can he hold a conversation with an adult? Does he have at least one good friend? Is he happy? If so then you have been a very, very successful parent.

If you can say yes to all of that you've done a fine job. The rest—finding a fulfilling life vocation, building a loving family, and whatever hopes and dreams you have for your child will take care of itself because you have provided him with the basic building blocks.

So my friends, stop worrying, you look fine, really. And yes, you are very, very good parent.

I REMEMBER YOU

Today while I was typing I made so many typos that I finally called Lilly in to the room to test me for a stroke. "Hey, when I smile do both sides of my mouth go up?" Yes she confirmed. "Tell me to raise my arms." She gave the command and I raised both my arms. I hoped. Yes, she nodded, I really did raise both arms.

Whew! Part of the reason I worry I might be having a stroke is because my mind does seem to be going a bit. I think it's because I'm in the "foggy years" of pre/menopause. At least I hope that's what's going on because if this is permanent it sucks.

My friend, umm, what's her name, uh we went to high school and I saw her last summer. Her name starts with an A and she used to live on Eight Mile and she had to miss our Halloween party senior year because she had an emergency appendectomy and she dated Bob K., you know, umm her name is, umm, Andrea. That's it. Andrea. I saw her for a mini-reunion last summer and she was telling us that she takes some pretty strong medication for arthritis with some unpleasant side-effects. She went to her doctor and said, "Hey this medicine is making my hair fall out and I can't remember words for you know, stuff."

The doctor nodded and said, "Well the medicine can make your hair fall out but it doesn't give you problems with word retrieval. That's your age. Studies show this peaks for women between about 49 and 51."

What a relief. Along with the typos and the forgetfulness and the word retrieval this stuff can get worrisome. I'm happy to blame it on a phase that will pass.

For some reason I have a lot of trouble with the word "pantry". I say to the kids, "Can you put this peanut butter in the um, you know it's like a shed but it has food," and finally one of them rolls his or her eyes and says, "Pantry, mom, pantry. You know this, you can do it," they say like they're trying to rehab a stroke victim, which I am not, as I proved earlier. Is that burned toast I smell?

I was talking about all this with my church lady friends today as we cleaned the kitchen after serving the Glenview clergy luncheon. (I totally just dropped that in there so you would be somewhat impressed with my goodness.) Anyhoo, I mentioned this word retrieval thing to my friends who are all around my age and my friend, umm, her name is, well it starts with an L and she lives over on that street next to mine and she got her MBA at Wharton. Now wait a minute, how is it I can remember she got her MBA at Wharton and I can't remember her name is Laura when I want to? Well she mentioned that she heard this word retrieval thing is worst with those words that mean, umm, they mean something like a person, place, or thing.

"Noun?" I supplied.

"Yeah, that's it."

So how weird is that? I mean we never forget the word "it" or "run" or "serendipitous" but just try to remember "pantry" or the name of someone I've known for years and forget it.

In the meantime when I run into you at Dominick's and it's clear I don't remember your name (and you apparently can't remember mine, thank God) please don't be offended. I DO remember that we were in book club together and that one time you brought the most awesome artichoke dip and your husband is kind of hot and works in advertising though I heard he was laid off and your kids are big jocks and you live over on the other side of town in that really nice house and you added the kitchen on a few years back and it's got a great granite island and when Lilly was sick you brought us chicken and rice (can I have the recipe?) and once when we made Margaritas you forgot to put the top on the blender and it blew all over my kitchen.

I remember all of this.

I just can't remember your name.

MINDFULLY NEGLECTFUL

The thing about trying to be an old-school, kids-should-not-be-the-center-of-our-universe, and-they-should-suffer-the-consequences-of-their-decisions, and-learn-to-be-self-sufficient parent is that sometimes other parents simply cannot allow it. Often when I have made a purposeful decision to allow my child to learn a lesson or take a more difficult path other parents mis-read the situation as a one-time error of omission on my part. But it's not. See, what they think is my accidental ineptitude is my deliberate neglect.

As an example, I like to allow my son to walk to and from his friends' home. To you this might seem like child endangerment but to me I think a 15-year-old who shaves can walk around the neighborhood. Even in the dark. But every time I arrange for him to do so, someone offers him a ride (to clarify, I mean someone he knows—if it were a stranger then my entire premise would be faulty).

Or the time he left his bike out on garbage day when he was in the first grade despite many warnings and it got picked up (fairly) by the scrap scavengers. When I told him I would not replace the bike a neighbor got wind of the story and dug out an old one for him from her garage. And when he wanted a new PS-Game-X-Thingy and I told him he'd have to wait until his birthday the mother of his friend bought him one thinking I could not afford one. She made an excuse, "I bought this for a friend and he didn't want it" but it was still in the package so I don't think so.

People, these are teachable moments. Work with me!

This kindness and generosity extends not only to the children around here but the parents as well. I never bring a camera (much less a camcorder) to school events. This is because I want to enjoy the event then capture it in my memory. That and the realization that no one, not even you, wants to see photos (much less videos) of your kids at school events. Sorry to inform you of this truth but not even the grandparents (especially the grandparents) wants to suffer through this crap despite anything they may have said to the contrary. In fact, not even the kid at the event wants to see the photos or the videos. No, not once has one of my kids said, "Hey Mom, do you have a nice clear shot of me playing the clarinet in the fourth grade winter concert?" And I am fairly sure that no kid has ever come home from college and said, "Mom, can I borrow the video of me in the fifth-grade play, I want to show it to all the guys in the dorm." So, while I attend all my children's events, I do not record them for history. But this for some reason, makes other moms very uncomfortable. On more than one occasion a very nice, and well meaning mom has leaned over and said, "I see you forgot the camera. That happened to me once," then snapped pictures of my kids and emailed them to me. I am not making that up.

And I just remembered the time when I was snack mom for a soccer game and had not had a chance to get to the store. Screw it, I thought. The little rats can go a whole hour without fruit roll-ups and granola bars. But when I got to the game and ran into a friend from the neighborhood and told her what was going on she blanched. No, she could not allow this. She got on her bike and rode home for granola bars and juice boxes. She did this not because she felt the little tykes on the field needed snacks, no, she did this to save me. (In hindsight it was a good thing too because I don't even know what the social consequences of "failure to bring snack when you're snack mom" are—I've never seen it in 16 years.)

I believe someone once said (maybe it was me) that when it comes to parenting anyone who does more than you do is obsessive and anyone who does less is neglectful.

So please don't think I'm neglectful—I'm deliberately doing less.

That sounded a lot better in my head than it looks on paper.

YOUR SOMEDAY TATTOO

Tattoos have become so mainstream that just about anyone under the age of 50 has their someday tattoo in mind even if they don't actually have a tattoo. I realized this last weekend as I ran into a friend at Borders and when she asked what we had planned for the evening and I told her we were going downtown to get Jeff a tattoo she did NOT say, "Really, you know employers frown on that sort of thing," nor did she say, "Do you know how saggy that's going to look some day?" which are both silly things I've heard old people say about tattoos. Instead she said, "Oh, if I ever get a tattoo it will be the iron man symbol and it will go right here," and she showed me the spot on her arm where she would put her someday tattoo. I should point out she is a banker, not a biker.

Jeff has also had a someday tattoo for some time; musical notes on the inside of his forearm that he could see when he looks down the neck of his guitar. I've encouraged him to turn this vision into reality but so far the opportunity to get a tattoo had not presented itself—until last weekend when the bunny shelter that Lilly volunteers at had a fund-raiser at a local tattoo parlor. Yes, for two days, all the proceeds of all tattoos and piercings would go to the shelter. At last, an excuse for Jeff to get his tattoo (that and his 50th birthday is right around the corner and you've got the perfect storm).

Which is why last Saturday night while our two eldest children were otherwise occupied with the annual high school variety show production, Lilly, Jeff, and I drove into the city. We brought Lilly because even though she is only 11 it is after all her charity.

The place was located in a not-so-gentrified part of town. Inside it was well-lit and set up like a Hair Cutlery. There were several 20 and 30-somethings sitting on benches waiting to get inked and most already had some visible tattoos. As the old suburban couple with a child we definitely looked a little out of place. I approached the counter and a Zooey Deschanel (with black hair not blonde like in Elf) look-alike took our information down and assured us that the wait was not too bad—half an hour. Oh goody, plenty of time to people watch. Lilly grinned happily because people watching is one of her favorite hobbies.

We sat and watched the comings and goings. The tattoo artists themselves were working on various body parts in chairs separated by curtains but all the curtains were open so we could watch. There was a woman wincing in one corner as the inkman bent over her back. I caught her eye and it was clear she was in pain. Zooey came and asked Jeff what he wanted done and Jeff showed her the photo he had brought. She asked about size and placement and then went to make a transfer of it. She said Tom would be doing the work. We had already seen Tom and were fascinated with his full-arm tattoo that was basically a colored dark green solid sleeve from wrist to elbow (picture above).

Lilly was wearing one of her bunny t-shirts (she has an extensive collection) so that sparked some conversation with the other customers. It seems that nearly everyone waiting was there to get a tattoo of a bunny or a bunny paw prints. They all talked bunny talk for some time and then Tom approached us holding the transfer. "So, who is this for?" he asked looking at all three of us. I nodded toward Lilly and dead-panned, "Her." Tom waited a beat. Blinked. Then said, "Cool."

I laughed and said not really and the others sitting there laughed with relief because really, a tattoo may be mainstream but no one wants to see an eleven year old with her parents getting one on a Saturday night. I mean really. I may TAKE my kid to tattoo parlor but I wouldn't let her GET a tattoo! What kind of mother do you think I am?

Tom had us follow him back to his chair. He put the transfer on Jeff's arm and wet it (think fake tattoos your kids get at birthday parties) and made sure Jeff liked it. He did, so Tom started the tattoo basically filling in where the stencil was. Now for those of you who have never seen a tattoo the way it works is that a little electric needle pokes multiple holes in your skin and the ink goes into the holes. It does not go deep but it IS a needle poking holes in your skin so it smarts a bit. Jeff was stoic and did not cry. He even watched.

I chatted with the girl across the aisle who was getting her 6th tattoo — a rather large memorial to her grandfather on her calf. She was friendly enough and mentioned her mother hated tattoos. I realized I was probably about the same age as her mother but I kept that thought to myself and I showed off my own tattoo (the outline of a heart on my hip which you can only see if I'm in a bikini) and she acted properly impressed.

Turning back to Jeff's tattoo man I noticed he had two certificates posted on the wall above him. One was verifying that he had the proper credentials to ensure no one would get an infectious disease from him and the other was "Best in Bible Verse Memorization for the Neighborhood." I found both certificates impressive and reassuring. By then Tom was done and carefully put a bandage on Jeff's arm. The whole thing took no more than five minutes. We went and paid Zooey and that was that.

So there you have it. Getting a tattoo is now as mundane as going to the movies or out for dinner and takes less time than a haircut. The people there were friendly. No one was drunk and not one sailor or biker entered the salon the whole time.

Maybe you have a someday tattoo—you know what it would be and where it would go. Maybe you "almost got one" but were talked out of it (yes TJ, I mean you). Now that you know how easy it is maybe it's time you go get one because let me tell you if you get one in an out of way place it will not interfere with your job prospects and if you're worried about a saggy tattoo —well you're going to be saggy some day with or without the tattoo.

How about it? Is today someday?

STAY AT HOME MOMS and USED CAR SALESMEN

Hey fellow stay-at-home moms, good news, there's a new movie about our wacky, unfulfilled, stressful lives out there! It's called *Motherhood* and it stars Uma Thurman (who ironically, is a working mom in real life). In the article I read, the women who wrote, produced, and star in it discuss how they are uniquely qualified to make a movie like this because men just wouldn't know what it's like to be a stay-at-home mom.

But then it goes on to say that none of them are stay-at-home moms either. According to the *New York Times* article:

"All the women who created *Motherhood* have made different life choices from Eliza (the main character), in that they have all stayed in the work force and risen to positions of power. 'For all of her angst the fact remains that Eliza has the option of not working,' said Rachel Cohen, head of production for the iDeal Partners Film Fund, one of the producers of the movie and a mother whose son is 5. 'I didn't have that option, and if I did, I think I would still want to work'. They work, the creators agree, because they fear becoming their lead character, who has metaphorically lost her voice and is struggling to figure out what to say about the choice she has made."

Err, excuse me?

Is there any career more horribly depicted in our culture than stay-at-home moms? Always shown as petty (New Christine), over-sexed (Desperate Housewives), depressed (Mad Men), and/or harried (Everybody Loves Raymond).

Maybe used car salesmen. I guess I have never seen a movie or TV show that showed the upside and fulfillment of that job but it, like any other job, has its ups and downs, its joys and sorrows.

Just once I'd like to see a stay-at-home mom on TV or in the movies that looks just a little like the smart, funny, kind, extremely generous moms who I know. Moms who look great in a pair of jeans, garden like Martha Stewart, and offer to watch kids when you're sick. Women who were once lawyers, business execs, and teachers who left it behind to do endless loads of laundry in exchange for the privilege of being present for every first step, new tooth, and birthday party. Moms who clean up every drop of puke, pee, and blood from every one of their blessed offspring. Who read *Green Eggs and Ham* a thousand times and then read it again. Great women who run church fundraisers and make meals for sick neighbors. Good friends who always know when you need a cup of coffee to discuss the latest child worry , or a glass of wine to celebrate a small rite of passage. Amazing women who know how to turn hydrangeas pink, install a light fixture, and get mud out of white pants.

But I guess the truth just doesn't make good TV or movies.

In fact, now that I think of it, there a few groups of women who are as maligned in the movies as stay-at-home moms—it's working moms (who are always shown as torn between two worlds) and career women (who all allegedly lust after babies).

I guess the message from our culture is clear then: no matter what you're doing—you will be ridiculed.

So here's to all of us- moms and childless, working and staying home. We're all terrific—we just aren't funny movie characters.

47, 48, 49 OBLIVION

They just said on the radio that the new H1N1 vaccination is being recommended to everyone between the ages of 2-49. And this morning I read in my beloved New York Times that The Big Bang Theory does well in the coveted 18-49 year old viewing demographic. And just now when I took a parenting magazine survey and they asked my age the final two categories were 45-49, 50 and older.

So what, you might ask? Well, I happen to be 49 and now realize I am on the verge of demographic obsolescence. This comes as a great surprise to me and perhaps even more so to my parents in their 70's and my grandmother who is 94. Really? Really, America you decide that anyone over 49 is no longer demographically significant? Soon you will no longer waste flu vaccines on me or care what I'm watching on TV or how I parent my kids?

This is especially funny to me when I consider that based on family history I will probably live another 49 years and will be watching more and more TV as I age AND that I have a whole lot more discretionary income than I did when I was 18. But do advertisers care what I watch? Well, yes, they do for another eight months but then it will be all, "Oh, you're 50 so you can't be cool anymore and we don't care if you watch Glee and MadMen because you're old."

Fifty? When did fifty signal the end of life? I mean, when since the medieval times when we all had babies at 12 and lost our teeth at 30 and died at 40, did 50 mean old? Whatever happened to that line "Merry Christmas to kids from 1 to 92" (I often wonder what my grandma thinks when she hears that line. I guess she has to acknowledge she is no longer a kid).

It is not fun to have to check the last box on a survey especially when it comes to age. Though, come to think of it, it is not fun to have to check the last box for a few things like marital status: (single, married, divorced, seeing someone, it's complicated, please mom get off my back, married in some states but not most).

With other categories it might be fun to check the last box say the one for educational level (high school, some college, college, some post-grad, graduate degree, PhD, good god are you EVER going to stop going to school?) or the income level boxes (0-$20,000 a year, $25,000-$40,000, $40,000-$65,000, $65,000-$100,000, $100,000 to more than anyone really needs).

It's getting so I am a little embarrassed to have to check that age box at all. Sometimes when I'm filling out forms in the doctor's office, I let my hand hover near the top of the list in case anyone is watching (which reminds me of the game we used to play at University of Michigan when we'd go see our grades posted—since they posted them in the order from 4.0 to 0.0 with our student ID number next to them we would all tilt our heads up as if looking at the top of the list while our eyes scanned down the list until we finally came to our actual grade—I nearly gave my eyes a hernia trying to keep my head up to see my calc grade).

Anyhoo, I am digressing. Back to the old age thing. I think it is kind of weird that Letterman who is 62 and Leno who is 59 are chasing after the 18-49 year old viewers (though not as weird as chasing after that age group in the office—bah-ding-bang!).

Maybe I'll write to the TV station and complain about this age-ism. But I better hurry because in eight months my letter will just end up in the "50 and over" pile.

PRENATAL TO PROM

In 1993, just during this time of year, I was four months pregnant with Atticus. I went to meet our real estate agent who was trying to sell our condo in Barrington (which is another story all together).

I got out of my car and she got out of hers, and she turned slowly to face the late afternoon sun and squinting at my baby bump she smiled and pointed at me,

"Watch out. One minute you look like that, and the next you're going to help him pick out his prom tux," which is what she had just been doing prior to meeting me there.

Now this is a sentiment all parents have heard many times and it was not the first time I had heard it and certainly not the last. But it is the time that sticks with me the most; I think because she said it without sentiment, without regret, but simply as an irrefutable fact in the same tone you might say "The sun has always set in the west," and I know I felt a chill run up my spine on that warm May night because I got it. I really got it.

I used to be slightly annoyed with this kind of advice because really, what can you do about it anyway? Are they telling me I should try to slow time down? Well, that's how I interpreted it for a long time and I really did try. Mightily.

In fact when I listened to Joni Mitchell's Circle Game (yes, I know I've referenced this song before) I would wait to hear the milestone that most closely marked my eldest child's time with me and I would feel triumphant if we hadn't gotten there yet.

Yesterday a child came out to wonder. Caught a dragon-fly inside a jar and I'd think, "Yes, he still does that!"

Skated over ten clear frozen ponds "Yes! He's only nine! Lots of time left"

This is delusional behavior and maybe even slightly psychotic and it did not work. Time did not slow down. In fact, it sped up and before I knew it, ***cartwheels turned to car wheels round the town.***

And today is senior prom and I remember Deb Villers saying that to me all those years ago.

And I thought about it as we picked out Atticus's tux this week (white dinner jacket, black pants, yellow vest and tie to match her dress, thanks for asking.)

And I thought about what that advice really means. Because of course it does not mean "Be careful time goes fast, try to slow it down." It means "It goes so fast so enjoy, embrace every minute. Savor every peanut-butter and jelly kiss, every night up in the bathroom with the shower steaming for a croupy cough, every god-awful honking squeaking band concert, and every psycho teen-aged melt-down. Because it does go crazy fast but it is also crazy fun and worth it all."

For new moms everywhere (shout out to Leslie who is in that photo above) —you cannot slow the circle down.

But you can enjoy every single spin you take around it.

CONFIRMING I'M AN IDIOT

Last weekend my Atticus (14) and Grace (12) were confirmed at our church. Also, I had been a mentor to another confirmand, Amanda, so I was involved as both a parent and a volunteer. The event, as big events often do, served as a microcosm of all that is good and bad about my skills in both areas. Mostly what is bad come to think of it.

I like to hang loose, not over-plan, not over-do things. I like to fly by the seat of my pants and not sweat the details. All of which make for a good surf bum but a fairly inadequate parent and church volunteer. I was actually fired from Sunday School duty a few years back. Well, not fired, but not asked back which is the same thing.

The confirmation process is designed to educate the youth of our church so that they can accept their faith freely. This is a bunch of hooey of course. What 12-year-old has the life experience to accept one religion over another? Still, we push forward with this tradition and accept that on occasion the plan backfires. As it did with my son who announced a week before confirmation that he was having serious doubts about his faith. In fact, he decided he might want to be a Buddhist.

Umm, errr, well yes, it's all well and good to seek God wherever he or she may be for you but we just don't want you to do that in the eighth grade.

What the hell kind of message is that? The kind I gave him. After much talking about it he agreed to go forward with the process as a sort of family tradition and I hope was able to do this in fairly good conscience.

The night before confirmation there was a banquet for the confirmands, their parents, and the mentors. I was there as both a parent and a mentor. I vaguely remembered reading an email that said we would be called upon to speak about our confirmand. No sweat, I thought, I can say a few words about Amanda. So imagine my surprise, when upon finishing dinner a microphone was produced and all the mentors pulled out lengthy speeches they'd written about their confirmands. "Umm, did we know we were supposed to do this?" I asked Grace's mentor who was sitting next to me going over her notes, "Actually, yes we did," she said, unwilling to give me a pass.

Okay, well, I'm pretty good on my feet I thought, I can pull this off. Then the first person gave a speech. This speech was just slightly more poetic than the Gettysburg Address and nearly as inspiring as the "I Have A Dream" speech. But with more Bible verses. Holy crap. There was no way I was going to be able to pull this off. Jeff, who was enjoying my squirming leaned over, "Your only hope is to go now and throw yourself at the mercy of the crowd!" he hissed. "No," I said, "I'm sure I'm not the only one ill-prepared," and I waited it out sure there would be someone as irresponsible as me.

But no. I really was the only one without a thoughtful prepared speech. What did I think? You take your crowd of church people who are asked to be mentors and you've got a fairly responsible group (not sure how I got in there). When it was my turn I mumbled through it forgetting a few details like saying anything nice about my confirmand or the whole process, then sat down and looked around the room to see if the torture was over. No. It was not. Because now all the mentors began to produce small wrapped packages to give to their confirmands. All except me (I did have a card) and Grace's mentor who said, "I have a gift for you. I'll bring it tomorrow." Oh sure, I thought. She has to figure out what to get still, just like me.

That's how I happened to be at Target last Saturday night buying the last cross necklace in the jewelry case.

Anyhoo, on Sunday morning when I presented the necklace to Amanda I was feeling pretty smug. A lot of the confirmands got the same thing so I was pretty sure I'd pulled it all out of the tailspin. I was curious to see what Grace's mentor had scrounged up the night before. I hadn't seen her at Target. Maybe she had to get beef jerky from 7-11, ha, ha!

Grace opened her gift. There was a small silver jewelry box with a Bible verse engraved on the lid. Inside the box was a silver cross with her name engraved.

Lilly leaned over and whispered, "I don't think she got that at Target last night, Mom."

Well, I'm happy to report that the rest of the day went smoothly. We got Grace and her Buddhist brother confirmed, for better or for worse and I was able to pull off my final duties as a mentor (stand up when they confirmed Amanda) without screwing it up too badly (my shirt was half tucked into the back of my pants).

I think, however, I will not be asked to mentor again so I can add to my list of dubious distinctions having been fired as both a Sunday School teacher and a Confirmation Mentor at the Methodist church.

Maybe the Buddhists would take me.

NamasteLorem Ipsum

PART 02: KIDS

AS THE NEST EMPTIES

The thing I did not realize about this whole empty nest thing is how it happens in stages over a really long period of time. Unless you have an only child of course, but for those of us with two or more, it is not an all-or nothing prospect. I mean, all your kids don't just get up and move out of the house one day and you and your husband are left alone.

No. Just as you did not fill the nest all at once you do not empty the nest all at once either.

And just as each child changed the dynamics and the nature of your household when you brought him or her home from the hospital, the same thing will happen as each one moves out to whatever is beyond life at home full-time.

Left behind will be a new, changed family.

The more kids you start out with on the front end, the more new families you get to parent on the back-end.

I first noticed this last fall when Atticus left and things were different right away. For example, I could keep up with laundry for the first time in years. And if I made a girly meal with things like quinoa and kale in them, no one said, "Umm, did you make meat with that?" and when we went to restaurants and hotels we found life was a lot easier getting a table or a room for four instead of five.

I found I talked a lot more to Grace than ever before. I have to admit, Atticus had been my go to guy for conversation for some simple reasons: he was there first and when the girls came along he was the first to move to the front seat next to me as we drove through life so I just talked to him more.

This is probably typical for the oldest but it does mean the second just doesn't get the time to talk to mom as much.

Until the oldest moves away.

With Atticus gone I was free to talk to Grace and get to know her better. I liked her very much and realized there are many upsides to emptying the nest little by little.

Also, last year for the first time she was the oldest Ludwig at school and she finally had a chance to shine as she found herself out from under the long shadow her big brother has always cast.

It was a delightful year to watch her blossom then bloom.
The same thing happened to her relationship with Lilly: with the two of them left as the only kids, they grew even closer and it was great fun to watch as they explored life as two teen girls kind of owning the place (and the car!) together.

Their new life involved a lot of Starbucks trips and clothes sharing and at first a little more squabbling than normal (because it turns out big brother also served as a buffer) but ultimately less squabbling as a new equilibrium was established.

I started thinking about how this phenomenon must affect other families in the neighborhood who surely have experienced this same thing—the ever-changing family and the affects on the left-behind sibs. Like neighbor, Carrie O., mother extraordinaire of four kids.

She has two girls close in age and then two boys close in age. So when I first met her, in the mid 90's she had two girls and a new baby, and her house was a girly house and her girls dressed like girls from a girly house. They were rather famous for their FABULOUS giant, crisp white hair-bows and we all found it impressive because we struggled just to keep our girls' hair combed decently, let alone adorned with a big, clean white bow.

But last year, her second daughter went off to college. And her house became a house of all boys; the kind of house where you don't serve a lot of smoothies and I'll bet it's been some time since Carrie opened a drawer and found it full of white bows.

And I imagine sometimes it is weird to Carrie that she started with an all-girl house but ended up with an all-boy house.

As I said, this also affects the kids left home. I think of my friend Kelly, whose youngest, Charlie, has grown up as the youngest boy of four. He has only ever known what it's like to be the mascot of a giant fun frat-house complete with all sporting activities and multiple trips to the ER. But some day, in the not too distant future, he will wake up and find himself not the part of a great raucous clan but—an only child! And he will remain the only child for several years. And how weird will that be?

I know Lilly is not looking forward to being an only child but here it comes. Because when the house changes next week, she will go from having been the baby for 14 years to being an only child.

Now there may be kids out there from larger families who look forward to being the only kid in the house but I have yet to meet one. Most of them are perfectly fine having run in the shadow of an older sib with little parental scrutiny. And they are not looking forward to having that cover ripped off.

Lilly dreads it.

So now, in addition to dealing with the grief –and I don't think that is too strong of a word to describe what she will feel when Grace goes to school— she will have to deal with the fact that her father and I look at her each night at dinner and ask her, and her alone, what happened at school that day. And there will be no one else to answer that question.

This past week, we were up at my parents' home in Michigan for an end of summer visit. Neither Atticus nor Grace could join us so Lilly invited her best friend Lauren to come along. Now Lauren, as it turns out, is an expert at being an only child. She has been one for her entire 14 years and likes it quite a bit, thank you very much.

She even tried to help Lilly out. "Watch and learn," she said. "I've been doing this a long time and I am going to teach you how to do it." She tried to show Lilly the fine art of eavesdropping on the adults during cocktail hour. But man, Lilly had no game at all.

The girls sat playing Uno while we visited. I could see Lauren was half-listening but I could also see Lilly was actively NOT listening to us.

At one point, I saw Lauren's ears pick up when we got to some juicy family gossip. Lilly continued to ignore us. I made eye contact with Lauren whose face was saying, "I know can you believe she just missed THAT?".

After a few days of pointing out the benefits of being an only child without Lilly picking up any of it Lauren threw in the towel. "I see you have much to learn before you appreciate what you're about to be given."

So that's where we are. It's August, the nest will be two-thirds empty as of next weekend, I will be the parent of an only child for the first time, and Lilly is not even trying to embrace her impending only-childhood.

But just as we found much of the upside as the nest emptied of our first, I hope to find the upside of having Lilly as an only child.

And I know that some day, Charlie will also find much to love about at last being the center of his parents' universe. Most of the time.

Best of luck to us all this month as many of our nests empty a little or a lot.

SHOPPING FOR BIG BROTHER

Yesterday Atticus (who was home for Easter) spent most of the day in his boxer shorts. He did put pants on when Grace's boyfriend, Billy came in. I said, "Hey maybe even a shirt?" and he glanced down at the pile of clothing on the floor and said, "Oh, yeah, here's a shirt."

I should mention the pants he did put on were pajama bottoms my mom made him for Christmas because he prefers a sort of lounge-wear look.

Later, as we set the table for Easter dinner he said, "I think I'll put regular pants on," and went upstairs to change into jeans. He did this on his own. So proud of my big boy.

His baby sister commented, "Hey, you're wearing big-boy pants. They look good. Did I pick those out for you?"

"Yep."

To say my son does not care about clothing is clearly an understatement. There was, as you may recall, the unfortunate 7th grade incident in which he accidentally wore his sister's jeans to school. Perhaps that is why he prefers pajama bottoms now. Yes, that's it—it's not that he's a lazy slob—it's because he suffers from PTSD. And there's the fact that he doesn't wear (or even own anymore, I stopped buying them) a winter coat despite the fact that he goes to college in downtown Chicago but that perhaps is another blog altogether.

Anyhoo, over Christmas break I asked his sisters to take him shopping. "Buy him some new jeans and maybe a shirt that is NOT a black t-shirt with an ironic saying."

The girls leaped at the chance to play "What Not to Wear" (which is our FAVORITE show) and one afternoon, when I was not feeling well, they grabbed the credit card and their brother and took off to the mall.

While they were gone I got a frantic text from Grace, "He has NO idea what he's doing. He does not even know how a dressing room works." Hmm, maybe all those years I ran into Kohl's and grabbed two pairs of jeans and three new shirts for him while he was at school did not serve him well in the real world. For him, that was the extent of his "back-to-school" shopping.

They came home successful. The girls proudly showed me their acquisitions. Two pairs of jeans that were actually in fashion (as opposed to the carpenter jeans he's been wearing for four years), a few nice shirts and even a cardigan sweater.

Then they showed me the two tops they had bought themselves as a "reward" for their trouble. Ahem. I had to reiterate the house rule that all unauthorized purchases must be returned or mom must be reimbursed.

It was a full month later I got Atticus's version of events. He told me his sisters were ruthless and even—get this— MADE HIM TRY THE CLOTHES ON! The nerve. He begged them not to try anything on but then, as he tells it, "Grace got those crazy eyes and said Mom would not pay for anything if I didn't try them on. You know I do anything she says when she gets like that."

God bless Grace and her crazy eyes. If you know her well you've seen them. Wonder if Billy has seen those yet?

I digress. The point is, well as usual there is no real point, it's just funny but let's say the point is this—when you have kids it's fun to get the ones who like to do something to make the one who doesn't like do something do it. (Ha ha, I can just see Laurent my English as a second language friend puzzling over that awful sentence). Then you can just lie on the couch until you feel better.

And in the end, you might have someone who voluntarily changes from pajamas to jeans for a semi-formal dinner.

Baby steps.

THE KISSING HAND

Each year, the night before school begins, I read the book *The Kissing Hand* to each of my children. In case you are not familiar with this sadistic book, it is a children's story about a raccoon who is scared to go to school until his mother gives him a kiss on his palm and explains that this symbolizes that her love will be with him no matter where he goes. There is not a mother in the world who can read this book aloud to her child without crying and I once saw a kindergarten teacher read it aloud to an entire room of parents and kindergartners on the first day of school with nearly disastrous results. No one likes to see grown men in suits sobbing.

Still, it is a tradition, and so I soldier on. This year, as I dusted the book off, I said to Lilly, "This year I will not cry," and I meant it. "Sure," she said, "Good luck with that."

I made it past the part where the raccoon says how much he just wants to stay home with his mommy because that no longer applies—she loves school and is happy to go. But when I got to the part where the mommy realizes she will miss her little raccoon I could not go on. I just pointed to the page and Lilly finished reading it for me.

With Atticus I made it all the way through. Teenage boys don't have much patience for their crying moms. But for some reason when I tried to read it to Grace I couldn't even start. I just had an image of her pleading with me not to send her to preschool. She just wanted to stay home. And I have to say, I should have let her stay home. Hindsight is 20/20 especially when it comes to parenting. Preschool is over-rated. Mandatory schooling starts soon enough. I started crying as soon as Chester said he wanted to stay home and Grace had to read the whole damn book to me, shaking her head in bewilderment as tears poured down my face.

As you go through your back-to-school rituals this fall with your own raccoons, from preschool to college, remember you are not alone. Despite the funny commercials showing the moms celebrating as the bus pulls away, we are all crying inside.

THE KISSING HAND: THE SEQUEL

Back to school means time to read "The Kissing Hand" that adorable story about Chester the raccoon who is scared to go to kindergarten until his mom gives him a special kiss on his palm to help him know she's thinking of him while he's at school.

It's a tear-jerker but I read it every year to each of my three kids the night before school. Except last night. I forgot my teens would be out until late and as they got home after I was already asleep I did not get to read it to them.

Which is why I was following my high-school senior around the kitchen this morning as he got his breakfast, reading aloud and trying not to cry as he tried not roll his eyes and laugh. I was doing fine but then I started thinking all of my friends who just took their freshmen kids to college—Ann who flew Olivia to TCU and Bridgette who is driving Billy to GVSU and Coop who took Nicholas to Clemson and Martha who drove Rachel to Miszou—and knowing I'm just a short year away from it all I started to cry a little.

As I angrily brushed tears away with the back of my hand I muttered, "I don't know why we all had you kids; all you do is grow up and leave us." And then I had to laugh and say, "Which I suppose is preferable to the alternative; that you grow up and don't leave us."

Lilly liked this idea and suggested a sequel to "The Kissing Hand" in which Chester moves back home after college and his mom pleads with him, "Please, I know we all have to do things that are scary but you'll be fine once you get an apartment of your own" just as she did when he was going off to kindergarten. Chester could be wearing boxers over his little ringed tail and scratch his belly and say, "But mommy, I don't want to leave you and the laundry you do for me and the meals you make!"

I don't know if the sequel would help any of us but it might be worth a chuckle.

To all of you having to say goodbye this month, my thoughts and tears are with you.

I'll be right there with you next year when my own raccoon leaves the nest.

HAND ME DOWNS

One of the great things about having kids who are too close together in age is that they can hand text books down to each other in high school. Why, you might ask, would that matter? Because, despite the fact that my kids attend a public high school with amenities such as a sushi bar and a rock-climbing wall, for some reason, I have to pay for their books to the tune of about $600 each kid each year.

So when the book list comes out I like to go through it and see which books we already have in the house. Of course, this is not as simple as one might hope. For one thing, the school likes to "update editions" rather frequently (how much can the World History book change in a year?) and apparently the teachers are sticklers about having the correct edition (are they getting a kick-back from Scott Foresman which happens to have its headquarters here in town?).

Sometimes, when I get real lucky I can reuse books we already had in the house even before we had kids. For Atticus, since he is a flexible kid, this works pretty well.

Me: Oh, *Great Gatsby*, I have that book!
Atticus: Okay.
Me: Hmm, but it says you need the 2007, hard-cover, annotated version . I think I have the 1977 totally dog-eared version.

Atticus: Who cares? It's not like anyone has re-written the story.

Unfortunately, Grace is not so flexible. Instead we have conversations like this.

Me: *Catcher in the Rye*! We have three copies of that. (and I go fetch them all)
Grace:(inspects them all and declares) I need a new one.
Me: WHAT?
Grace: It has to be the newest, rack-size version and this one has the wrong cover, this one is the wrong size, and this one is right but Atticus has already written notes in it and I have to turn it in so the teacher can check our notes.
Me: They should not be encouraging you to write in books.
Grace: I need to buy a new one.
Me: Forget it. Your choices are to use the wrong size or the pre-noted version.
Grace: I can't use the wrong size! When she says we have to read pages 23-47 it won't line up!!!
Me: And you can't figure that out? Fine, if you need a fourth copy of *Catcher in the Rye*, you can buy it yourself.

That was the end of it it I thought until driving to school the other day when Grace said, "Atticus, I cannot figure out why you circled this sentence and I had to make up a reason for my teacher."

"What sentence?" he asked. She read it aloud.

Thus ensued a spirited discussion on Holden Caulfield and his propensity to label everything as phony and what exactly phony means anyway and I thought of the law of unintended consequences and decided that while reading a book and trying to explain why your brother circled certain passages is not exactly the assignment the teacher had in mind, it isn't the worst way in the world to discover a piece of classic literature.

And most of all I was glad to know we didn't need a fourth copy of *Catcher in the Rye* though it will be interesting to watch Lilly try to explain all the passages both her brother and sister circled.

TO KILL A MOCKINGBIRD

As someone who named her son Atticus, most people instantly know I feel strongly about the book To Kill a Mockingbird. *This week I have received emails from friends letting me know about various events being held to celebrate the 50th anniversary of the publication of the book. So I felt it was appropriate that I say a few words about the book and what it has meant to me.*

Growing up my father did not watch TV very much apart from the nightly news at 11:00. In fact, he watched it so seldom, I have clear memories of the few things he did watch. Here are the few things I can remember him watching— an episode of *Star Trek* that my (future film critic) brother dragged him in to the basement to see; *Wizard of Oz*—I sat on his lap during the scary parts; an episode of *Petticoat Junction* that my mom wanted to see because of a wedding (was that Bobbi Joe or Betty Joe?); the end of the football game that was famously interrupted by *Heidi*; the moon landing; and *To Kill a Mockingbird*. I knew instantly by the tone of voice he used when my mother told him it would be on that night that it was a very special movie indeed. I was only 8 or 9 and not surprisingly the movie did not hold my interest.

A few years later, at the age of 11 during one of those locust-like summer readings binges in which I ravaged my parents' library (and you know just what I'm talking about), I read *To Kill a Mockingbird* for the first time. I loved it instantly. I did not know exactly what rape was but I had an inkling and the themes of racial injustice, personal bravery, and loss of innocence, resonated with me. I was completely taken with the hero and father-figure Atticus Finch and have throughout my life continued to ask myself "What would Atticus do?" in times of moral dilemma. Quite recently an acquaintance mentioned that she had done that too and I suppose we are not the only two on the planet who have held Atticus in such high esteem.

I have never read *To Kill a Mockingbird* for a class, ironically. I have read it at least three times through but more often I pick it up and read a passage here and there. It never fails to delight—the story, the phrasing, the place and time, and above all the characters. So memorable you can recall them all easily, Jem and Scout, Miss Maudie, Boo Radley ... and many more you could name too I'm sure but above all Atticus.

Over the years I have read quite a bit about the book and how it came to be. For those of you who enjoyed the book but perhaps haven't delved in to the topic as deeply, I offer some trivia:

• The character Dill is based on Harper Lee's next-door neighbor, Truman Capote who did indeed come spend the summers with his aunt. His parents were horribly neglectful, father had abandoned them and mother was, for all practical purposes, a hooker who left him locked in hotel rooms while she went out to the bar. Some claim it is Truman Capote who really wrote *To Kill a Mockingbird* but there is scant evidence of that. Some also surmise that it is really Harper Lee who wrote the only good book Truman Capote published, *In Cold Blood* but that probably is not the case either. To be sure Harper Lee helped him research the book as no one in Holcomb, Kansas where the murders occurred wanted to talk to the pompous sissy boy from New York City. I can understand how they were good friends as children but often wonder how she put up with such a pretentious ass when she lived in New York. Maybe she didn't very well—they had a falling out at some point and were not speaking to each other when he died at 59 after drinking himself to death.

• Harper Lee was in her early 20's when she dropped out of law school and moved to New York to write. After struggling a few years with the age-old dilemma of trying to earn a living and finding time to write she was given a generous Christmas gift from friends—a year's salary and direction to quit working and write. She did and at the end of her year she had her masterpiece.

• Harper Lee hobnobbed with the New York glitterati for a few years. Helped Truman with his book and then seems to have had enough. She retired at a young age back to Monroeville Alabama and remains there, now in her mid-80's. She does not do interviews and as far as I know will have nothing at all to do with any of the anniversary events including the Monroeville County Presents: Celebration Weekend for To Kill a Mockingbird which, by the way, begins today.

• *To Kill a Mockingbird* is the only book she ever wrote. This makes a lot of people crazy (and some point to it as evidence that she did not even write it to begin with). But it doesn't bother me a bit. Why should she write another book after writing something so wonderful AND making sure it was turned respectfully into a weighty movie? Isn't that enough? I say thank you Ms. Lee for the gift and enjoy your peace and quiet.

Next up: On naming a kid Atticus and excerpts from the letter I have from Harper Lee!

TO KILL A MOCKINGBIRD PART II: THE NAME

When I was pregnant with our first child, Jeff and I decided on a boy name and a girl name but we did not tell anyone the names, fearing ridicule. Which is what lead to this endearing exchange in the hospital just after our son was born when my parents came to visit.

My mom: Oh my gosh he's darling! What's his name?
Me: Atticus.
My mom: (snort-laugh) No, really...?

I thought it was a great idea to name a child after a beloved literary figure — after all you would avoid the potential pitfalls of naming your child after a beloved historical figure only to find out later the figure was not exactly who you thought. Imagine the disappointment of that couple in "The Cosby" show who named their twins Winnie and Nelson, only to find out a few years later that Winnie was a big opportunistic ho. Well, I'm sure they weren't as disappointed as Nelson himself, but you get the idea.

So I thought a literary figure was safe. What I did not even consider, but now see nearly 17 years later quite clearly, was the possibility that I could name my kid after one of the most revered fictitious heroes of our time and then my kid could turn out to be an asshole. How stupid would that have looked?

Fortunately, I am quite happy to say my kid is not an asshole. In fact, I think he nicely embodies the spirit of Atticus Finch. Our Atticus is cerebral, and kind, and well beyond his years. Last summer, as many of you know, he asked to go to a Buddhist retreat in the Catskills where he meditated for hours. Really. As I write this he is in the city where he is taking a class in Sound Recording and one in Creative Writing at the Columbia College Summer High School program. He'll take the train home, something he's done on his own for some time.

So though it was a big risk, it turned out great. He loves his name and he loves that about half the world, upon hearing his name for the first time will ask, "Like from *To Kill a Mockingbird*?" (Apparently the other half never went to high school.) And he likes that the name is unique. There is only one other Atticus in Glenview—a boy three years younger who is as unique and cerebral as our Atticus, (and also a Buddhist). He does not mind sharing his name with him.

When he was born I wrote a letter to Harper Lee. I just addressed it to Miss Harper Lee in Monroeville, Alabama, not expecting anything but wanting her to know the name lived on. A few weeks later I received a letter from her—typed obviously on a typewriter. It is among my most prized possessions. (Of course, having said that, I have to confess that I have torn the house apart for two days and can't seem to find it, but it's here, of that I'm sure.)

(A bit off topic but regarding kids' names, I should mention that my girls both have heroic middle names. Grace's middle name is Imogene after the character Idgy in *Fried Green Tomatoes*, and yes I have a letter from the author Fannie Flagg. Lilly's middle name is Ruby, the only name we chose of a living hero, after Ruby Bridges, the girl who appears in a Norman Rockwell painting, accompanied by federal marshals as she integrated the New Orleans school system. And I have a lovely letter from her as well.)

So on this 50th anniversary of the publication of *To Kill a Mockingbird*, rest assured, the good name of Atticus lives on.

Even if Harper Lee's letter is temporarily misplaced.

TEENAGED BOYS: DELIGHTFUL

When I was pregnant with my first child (Atticus) I remember seeing babies and toddlers and thinking, "Awwww, I can't wait to have one of those!" One time I saw a teenaged boy ambling through the mall and I thought, "Wait! I DO NOT want one of THOSE!"

So I am glad to report that now that I have one of THOSE in my house it is really quite delightful.

Teenaged boys are straight forward and tell you what they're thinking. They are hilariously funny and celebrate the absurd. Though they may not put a lot of thought into your birthday present, they are sweet and still wipe tears away from their little sisters' cheeks. And they can program the phone/tv/dvr or fix any technological problem you might have. As I type this he's installing a new cooling system on the PC downstairs. Whatever that means.

My teenaged boy is quirky (go figure) in addition to all those other things. He sees auras. He mentioned this quite casually once a few years back. "My music teacher has orange light around her." He is curious about everything and as an avid fan of the history channel knows something about almost everything. Lately, he's been bringing me up to speed on the whole North Korea Kim Dong Il thing. But he's just as likely to launch into a discussion on medieval weapons (do you know the difference between a cudgel and a shillelagh?) or the likelihood that Nostradamus's predictions are accurate.

He is a "serial-interest-taker". He has an interest, he learns all he can about it, he often saves up and buys one, then he moves on. Accordion, ocarina, Rubiks Cube, tarot cards, and yo-yos come to mind. He dedicates hours of time on the internet learning about these things and teaching himself how to use them with YouTube.

Unfortunately, he seldom (no wait, NEVER) brings this passion, curiosity, and devotion to his schoolwork.

Which is why he was getting bad grades this spring and we were moved to ground him from his computer games and from his beloved stage crew (another of his passions—as a Freshman he has been given light and sound board duties normally reserved for Seniors). With all this free time we had hoped he would apply some of it to his homework.

But alas, he has squandered his extra time on the latest of his serial interests: painting. Yes, he used his free time and hard-earned money, to passionately pursue this. He saw the now-deceased Bob Ross on PBS. (In case you do not know who this is, I will explain, he is an extremely odd, charismatic guy who teaches people to paint on TV). Bob Ross believed anyone can paint. Atticus believes that too. So while he was supposed to be spending this spring raising his math grade he's been standing next to the computer (he downloaded the show) paintbrush in hand, following Bob's direction.

So if you have a baby boy and are not so sure about the whole teenager thing, don't worry. It will be great. He will have his own interests and passions even if he doesn't have good grades. And like all children, if you let him, he will show you a world you did not know exists.

And if you're lucky, you might get some new paintings for the living room.

8TH GRADE GRADUATION

Yesterday Grace delivered a speech she wrote at the eighth grade awards ceremony. Since I have writer's block this week I am going to publish her speech which allows me to take a break from my own writing AND brag on my kid. It's a two-fer! I hope you enjoy this as much as I did! Attea, by the way, is the name of Grace's school.

The Alphabet of Attea

by Grace Ludwig

Attea is like the alphabet. Many letters, or people in Attea's case, make up a whole. Each one is different, and contributes in their own way. Some people, and some letters, speak out often, and others only shine once in a while. A few choose to make their appearance only when brought together with another person or letter, and others want to be left alone. Attea is an alphabet in its own way.

A is for awesome. If I could describe Attea in one word, I would choose awesome. Attea is awesome for many reasons, all of which you will hear within the rest of the alphabet.
B is for boring. Yes, occasionally the learning part of school can get a bit boring.

C is for choir, band, and orchestra. I know not every student participated in these activities, but I can name many occasions when my friends and I laughed at Mrs. Reatherford pretending to be mad at us, or Ms. Monastaro's juicy stories.

D is for drama. And I don't mean in just Mr. Luongo's class. I'm talkin' boys asking girls out, break ups and makeups, friend fights and more, all of which you can find in the halls of Attea.

E is for education. After all, to get an education is the reason we go to school in the first place!

F is for friends. I cannot even begin to name all the amazing friends I have met and had great times with at Attea.

G is for gym class. I would be the first to tell you I'm terrible at sports, so that's obviously not the reason I enjoyed gym class. What I enjoyed most was the laughs over missed baskets and un-caught baseballs.

H is for the hall way. I'm sure everyone has had some funny, strange, or even awkward moments in the hallway, and I'm positive these moments will continue throughout our years in high school.

I is for immature. Really? 8th graders are immature? You ask. But yes in fact, all 8th graders are immature. No matter how grown up or mature they seem to adults, every 13 or 14 year old has those funny thoughts in their head when a teacher says we need to complete our duties.

J is for the jokes and laughs that are always about the same thing but never get old.

K is for knowledge. The knowledge our teachers have is incredible, and we take advantage of it. Throughout my middle school years I have learned that not everyone knows as much as our teachers and they're only trying to share what they know with us.

L is for lunch. I will never forget the cafeteria and how we were all so convinced in 5th grade lunch would be so much more fun. It turns out; lunch was almost the exact same experience. It was very enjoyable, and will most likely be a similar experience next year.

M is for magnificent. Magnificent would be the second word I would use to describe Attea and all of the memories I have had here.

N is for new. In 6th grade, everything at Attea was new, to all of us. But now it is not so new, and we're all ready for new experiences and a new environment.

O is for Officer Smith. I will always remember Officer Smith, and the big kid he was on the inside even if he wasn't so much on the outside!

P is for potato chowder, which Mr. Woell enthusiastically presented to us during the announcements every week.

Q is for quick change. And not just changing into our gym clothes, but also adapting to our new schedule, lockers, teachers, and more.

R is for recess which included short but sweet moments with my best friends, usually taking place in the sun or woodchips.

S is for socializing. Students at Attea have wasted a large amount of time socializing. But school isn't just a place for learning; it's also a place to make friendships that could last for the same amount of time that you know your multiplication facts-forever.

T is for all the teachers I have had at Attea, which have taught me new skills and valuable lessons.

U is for unable to get enough sleep. If there is one thing I would go back and change, it would be to skip those late night Facebook chats and get a few extra minutes of sleep.

V is for victorious. All of us have conquered the battle of middle school, and are ready for a new challenge.

W is for hard work which, as 8th graders, we all deserve a little credit for, but instead we will gladly take the satisfaction of a good grade or score.

X is for x(ex)periences. The experiences I've had with everyone I've met at Attea have been good and bad, but I know through these experiences, I've been changed for the better.

Y is for the youth that will never grow out of us. I believe that every person over the age of 14 still has an 8th grade part of them on the inside

Z is for zero moments of unhappiness. We all have those days when you wake up feel like its going to be a bad day, but members of the Attea alphabet always help each other to feel excellent by 3 o'clock.

Attea is an alphabet. Teachers make up the most important letters, or the vowels, and students are like the consonants. Each letter is important and without it, the alphabet wouldn't be complete. But most importantly, Attea is like an alphabet, each letter is unique.

Beautiful Prom 2011

Perhaps you haven't been to a prom since the BeeGees had a top-ten hit. Or maybe you are so old you wore something called a Gunny Sacks to your prom (which is almost as ugly as a real gunny sack by the way). Or maybe you are a bit younger— a member of the Footloose generation and your kids are not yet going to proms. At any rate, I am here to tell you what a prom looks like these days, at least from a mom's perspective

As Grace is dating a Senior, she went to the Senior Prom last weekend and here's how things look these days, at least in our little corner of the world. Some of this is the same across the country I'm sure.

How he asks: It is no longer acceptable to sit next to a girl on the radiators (that's where we hung out at my high school) and say , "So, has anyone asked you to prom yet?" and then if the girl says "no" to say, "Want to go to prom with me?"

No no no my friend. Those days are over. Now, one must ask a girl to prom in a very creative and fun way. Skywriting is good. Texting is bad. An ad on a billboard is good. Calling on the phone? No way. Even sane girls (like my own) will insist a boy jump through this hoop. When her nice boyfriend Billy said, "So how do you want me to ask you to prom" (a ridiculously moot point as she had already bought the dress and isn't asking that question asking to prom?) she said, "You have to come up with something."

Yes, this is weird and kind of appalling to those of us who grew up in a simpler and more egalitarian age. But there it is. And that is why Billy was in our back yard on Easter morning laying out plastic eggs to spell something. He paused to consult the graph paper in his hand and Jeff looking out the window said, "What the hell? Doesn't the kid know how to spell prom?" Turns out Billy does know how to spell prom but having the heart of an engineer he had plotted the word out on graph paper to make sure he had enough eggs. Awwww. And in the golden egg he had written on a scrap of paper, "Will you go to prom with me?" so sweet. Of course she said yes.

The Dress: Well you know of course the girl must hunt for the perfect dress. That much has not changed. And you must have a dress that is unique—that has also not changed—and I was reminded of the subterfuge I was once a part of involving a dress shop that would not sell the same dress to girls from the same school and my going to buy a dress for a friend under an assumed name and I was not proud of that memory and I apologize to Karen Anderson. But anyhoo, today the girls have a more sophisticated technological way to deal with this problem. They set up a Facebook site called, "Don't steal my dress, slut" and they each post their dresses on there so no one will wear the same dress. Now it turns out that in this case, the term "slut" is an affectionate one. I guess this is like black people using the "n" word—because much to my surprise this is a kind and gentle site in which the other girls say things like, "Oh, that will look so good on you!"

and "I was going to get that but since you already have it I will buy a different one!" Don't believe everything you read about mean girls.

The dresses are still long. Some are quite umm, sophisticated. Some look like something Edyta from Dancing with the Stars might wear. No one wears lace collars and sleeves that cover every square inch of skin like we did. Thankfully.

The Tux: You will be shocked, shocked to learn boys no longer wear colored tuxes with ruffles that have been "tipped" to match their date's dress. About the wildest thing you'll see is a white tux. Thankfully.

The Venue: They still have proms at cheezy hotel ballrooms with mediocre food. This much has not changed.

The Groups: This is different. You NEVER go with just your date to prom. You must organize a large and unruly group of friends and acquaintances, many of whom do not like each other or hold grudges against each other. There will be angry texts and maybe even tears and lots of drama. And the girls are worse. In this way, you can actually find yourself rejected by a group even when you have managed to procure a date and asked her in a clever way. Whew! It's tough to be a guy these days. When Grace told me about some of the current drama I suggested she just go to the prom with Billy. She looked at me as if I had suggested that I go to the prom with her. So you see, the group is a must.

Limos and drivers and buses oh my: Because you are traveling in a pack of 20 or so kids, you can no longer go to the prom in you date's Pinto with the faux wood panels nor can you borrow his dad's Ford Fairlane. No silly, this will not do. You need a large vehicle that you and 18 of your closest friends will fit in. The kid in charge will wait til the last minute to book the vehicle and you will end up paying an exorbitant amount of money for a round-trip to the prom in a limo that looks like it has not been cleaned since the weekend before when it was used for a bachelor party that resembled The Hangover. If you are really lucky, you will get a surly, resentful limo driver who is not happy to be carting suburban children around town and he will take you to a dark part of the city and demand more money if you ever want to get home. This is called "a life lesson" and will make a great story for years to come. As a parent, you don't really mind any of this if it means you are not stuck driving the after after after prom party shift.

After Prom Activities: Prom never ends when it is over. It really lasts a whole weekend and there are trips to Great America or the Dells (Wisconsin's family version of Las Vegas) and jaunts to someone's lake house. A good friend who has an older daughter warned me about this. Her advice was to decide well in advance how much of this you can stomach and lay down the rules before all the planning begins. Which I did. No overnight trips I said, you are not even a senior. Then when your kid comes to you with a well-thought out plan and complex schedule involving responsible chaperones you can cave and let her go anyway. Which I did.

So there you have it. Prom 2011 is not a whole lot different from Prom 1978 as I see it. You still have a lot of young people dressing up like grownups for one night and lurching around on the dance floor to a DJ. Moms still ooh and ahh over their babies all dressed up for the night and take way too many pictures of their babies squinting into the sun.

And prom is still a night you never forget.

UPSIDE-DOWN DUCK

There was this time back in the 90s when I gave birth to three children in about four years. It was crazy, and chaotic, and wonderful and the only thing I would do differently if I had a do-over is I would have four children.

During that era I loved the challenge of the simple act of getting us all dressed and fed and out the door even if we were just going to the library. I liked knowing that if I did it all just right we made a peaceful and serene mother/children scene that made people smile—like a mama duck and her babies. And if I do say so myself, we looked pretty good most of the time.

I remember talking to my sister about how tricky it was to do that.

She said it was like being a duck: if you did it right, on the surface you were sailing along peacefully, your children calmly circling you—but underneath if anyone could see your feet you were paddling like hell.

Indeed.

Most of the fabulous mom friends I know are fantastic ducks. Or even swans (Ann R and Martha come to mind). They look amazing, they glide along, they look calm, their children now teens still glide along next to them peacefully and I love them and admire them for it.

And I know that this is not as easy as it looks.

I know that a lot of us (all of us at some time) are gliding along despite a broken webbed foot or a pond that is losing water rapidly. But we accept these challenges and work that much harder to glide.

Sometimes you might see a mom who is not so good at this.

I saw one yesterday at the Shedd Aquarium. She was there with two quiet school-aged kids but somehow she made it *feel* like she was herding a dozen screaming toddlers who needed naps and lunch.

It did not help that she had waaayyy too much gear: strollers, backpacks, lunchboxes, GameBoys—you get the picture. These types always have too much gear; sometimes they even have a spouse and they still look like they have no control over anything.

She was talking way too loudly, over-managing the kids, quizzing them to make the visit "educational", correcting them when it wasn't necessary and ignoring them when it was.

In short, she was making her own job much, much harder than it has to be. I thought "There goes a bad duck."

But later, when thinking more about it, I realized that this mom isn't just a duck who swims poorly, she is an ***upside-down duck***. She has her head under the water, her feet paddling madly in the air, flapping her wings beneath the surface nearly drowning, and making her children (and the rest of us) crazy.

If she just put all that effort and energy into paddling *under* instead of above the water she'd be sailing along.

So the next time you run into an upside-down duck (and you will) do us all a favor—tell her to TURN OVER.

We, and her children, will thank you.

GARBANZO BEANS AND TABLECLOTHS

To be a parent is to find yourself saying things you just never thought you'd say like, "You know you can't iron the tablecloth when it's already on the dining room table, right?" and to have one of your children look at you with that "duh" look but then say with not much conviction "Of course I know that!" only to later remove the tablecloth and find the very distinct imprint of an iron seared into the fine wood of your only piece of Ethan Allen furniture in the house.

It is also to come home from a nice dinner out with your husband to find strange things around the house like the above picture. You won't really know why that is there but you are pretty sure that one of your offspring constructed it for what seemed to be a very good reason at the time, not that it is a random piece of modern art. And perhaps when you go looking for your clipboard the next day you will find it inexplicably covered in aluminum foil.

Some how these things always crack me up although I know they are not always funny to everyone. My own mother would have had a heart-attack if she'd caught me ironing on the dining room table. For some reason, ruining wood (by spilling milk or not using a coaster or taping something to it) was about the most egregious act you could commit upon our house when I was a kid. I don't know why that was. Was wood more scarce then? Were people judged by the quality of their wood furniture? I don't know. I just know it was a crime in my home just shy of dripping candle wax on the bee-yoo-tiful red shag rug in the basement, the one that matched the Early American Bi-Centennial couch and lead to the now legendary story of my mother finding the said wax and pointing to it in horror saying in a tone of voice usually reserved for pedophiles, "CANDLE WAX!"

But I digress. I was talking about funny things you find around your house or find yourself saying like:

Me: Hey, who put an open can of garbanzo beans back in the pantry!
Child 1: What are garbanzo beans?
Child 2: I hate garbanzo beans.
Child 3: I don't even know how to use a can opener. You probably did it old lady!

All of which are salient points. Notice not one of them just said, "I didn't do that" (future lawyers?) and then you vaguely remember making a bean salad a few weeks before and deciding at the last minute to leave the garbanzo beans out of the recipe as Child 2 does indeed hate them and that quite possibly Child 3 is right and it was YOU who put an open can of garbanzo beans back in the pantry but you are also quite sure that before you had children you never did such things— so really, it IS their fault.

The morning after you have discovered the nail file taped to the desk and your aluminum-foil-clad clipboard one of your children will show you the fabulous video she made of herself playing the piano and you will be pleased and proud but most of all you will be happy to figure out that the nail file contraption was built to prop the iPhone up while it filmed her (though you still to this day don't know why your clipboard was covered in aluminum foil).

And that is why it is fun to be a parent because even when they are teenagers they will still be doing wacky things that confound you and amuse you —if you are not overly fond of your wood furniture and you don't really need your clipboard.

PART 03: SCHOOL

DISORIENTING

College orientation—for the parents—seems to vary greatly from school to school. After asking around I have heard everything from a parent who did not even know she was invited to orientation (her son's doing) to parents who go, stay in the dorm, attend a sample class, play quarter bounce with their underage kids and try to pledge a sorority. (All of that last one is true but the sorority).

Somewhere between these extremes lies my own experience now with two very different schools.

The Art Institute had a day of activity for the parents that mostly consisted of telling us how fabulous our artistic children are and that we were NOT crazy for paying for them to attend art school during the end of a depression. You can appreciate this is not an easy task for them but they were impressive and at one point I think they got the whole room to shout "The world needs more art not more lawyers" or some such nonsense that I actually believed for a second.

That was last summer.

This summer it was time for Grace to attend an overnight student/parent orientation at Valparaiso and we were invited.

I have to admit right here, I am not a fan of orientations. Anyones. Mine or my kids. Kindergarten through college. Don't like em. (And I actually ran the kindergarten one for a couple years).

Too much talking not enough information. Too many nervous parents spilling their fear all over me. Ick. Stop. I barely have it together myself without you raising things to worry about I never even considered!

But we go.

And there is ALWAYS "that woman" sitting behind me. I think she has followed me from Kindergarten orientation to college orientation. I mean this metaphorically, not literally. It is not the same exact woman but someone of her ilk.

You know the one. She is the one who will ask a question that is really a way to brag about her kid. She will frequently ask about the gifted program — when do they get tested? Does it extend into middle school?

In kindergarten she said, "My son already reads 'Harry Potter' books. What will he do all day?"

Sheesh.

The teacher was not new and blithely answered, "We have a lot of children who read Harry Potter books *and beyond*. And we have many who do not know their ABCs. I teach them all." We almost applauded her.

At Valpo, "that woman" sat behind me (by the way this is always a woman, I don't know why, but the dads don't ask this stuff) who wanted to know if her daughter's AP credits would count and how that worked. She asked THREE specific questions related to her daughter's AP classes and something called IB (this is apparently an Indiana thing, not a stomach disorder) and this was in a lecture of over a hundred people. Apparently, she thought it was a private counseling session and we were spectators.

I mentioned "that woman" at a neighborhood grad party recently. Everyone laughed because *everyone* has heard these "questions". One of the dads (who ironically has a brilliant child he COULD brag about but never does) said that at the "What to expect when your kid goes to college" seminar "that woman" asked the following: "My son never studies and has terrible organizational skills but he always gets all A's. How will he do in college?"

The lecturer should have just said, "Shut up."

Instead, he gamely tried to answer. I think it would be fun if he called her out on it and said, "Is this a real question or did you just want the chance to tell us your kid gets all A's without studying?"

Anyhoo, despite the questions from "that woman" the orientation was quite nice. We learned a few things and as is our norm, we skipped out early. This is our MO since we attended our first Lamaze class. The teacher went through the basics of childbirth (some details left me with my head between my knees) and then announced we would have a break. After the break, she said, the men will go in one room and the women will go in another and we will talk about our feelings. Jeff and I exchanged horrified glances, and without saying a word, left as soon as the instructor excused us for our break.

So after sitting through orientation lectures on Friday from 9 til 3 (and 5 more hours scheduled!) we skipped out and went back to the hotel.

This gave me the chance to have a mini-nervous breakdown about the fact that my daughter is leaving in the fall. Jeff helpfully suggested that getting a jump on my grief might make it easier in the fall, but I kind of doubt it.

So that's how orientation went for us. Grace got to meet her roommate for the first time, I got to get in an early cry, and we all got to hear about "that woman's" daughter who, if I understand it right, has enough credits going into college to skip to grad school.

As for how this compares to our own college orientation programs...well just like the whole process, I don't really remember my parents there at all. Were they even invited? One friend said she drove herself there. I think I might have too. I don't remember much about it except I thought everyone there was an arrogant ass and I had made a huge mistake choosing that school and cried myself to sleep in South Quad. Six weeks later I met the group of friends I still see annually.

If you are attending a college orientation this summer I hope you have fun and be sure to say hi to "that woman" as she will surely sit behind you too.

MOVING OUT OF THE DORM

Because my friends are such competent, capable, graceful handlers of complicated logistics, they seldom make a fuss over achieving something herculean and difficult like moving a kid out of a college dorm. No, I have never heard any of them really discuss in detail how much of a pain in the ass this process can be.

Like my friend Ann, who mentions oh so casually that she will be flying to Dallas, renting a van, dissembling a loft, finding a storage space for her daughter's belongings, packing up the clothes and flying home with her this weekend. She does not complain and makes it sound like anyone could pull this off in a weekend, *no problema*.

So I went blindly and foolishly to pick up Atticus from his dorm in the city on Friday. How hard could that be? I didn't have to fly anywhere or rent anything. Just drive down, fill up the car and drive home. Jeff offered to come help fill the car, then go in to work and take the train home. Even better! Easy peasy!

But when we got there, it turned out, nothing was easy or peasy.

I did not have ID on me (left it in the car, around the block in the parking garage) so the security guard at the front desk was pissed at me.

Atticus had lost his ID and his room-key the night before which meant he had not yet really gotten the administrative part of the moving process moving.

After looking through his stuff for half an hour we decided to give up on finding the key and ID and figure out how to move out without it. Think fees.

Now there was a waiting list for the moving bins so we began to move the crap ourselves by hand.

Three times we loaded ourselves up like Sherpas, waited forever for the elevator (he lives on the 15th floor) carried the stuff through the alley, past the three trucks and the forklift that were being used to load the entire set of the play "Big Fish" from the Oriental Theater that backs up to his dorm and the six smoking stage-crew guys, into the parking garage up eight flights (by elevator) and tried to cram it all in to Jeff's Lexus.

The fourth trip we scored a dolly and managed to put everything leftover on it. We cleaned up, Atticus met with the RA, discussed the fees due when one loses his key and ID on move out day and were good to go.

We pushed the elevator button and miraculously it opened up almost immediately.

Then the fire alarm went off.

Now as any good city boy knows, you do NOT get on an elevator when the fire alarm goes off. Atticus told us to drop everything and head down stairs. Which I did. At the 9th floor I realized Jeff was not with us. He texted: *It's a false alarm I am staying here. Elevators working, come back up.*

So Atticus and I turned around and trudged back up several floors.

Then the nice men from the Chicago Fire Department came running past us in full gear with their axes out.

We texted Jeff to get his ass out and headed back down a dozen flights with a gaggle of art students.

Standing around outside we watched the Fire Department come and go with little urgency. The kids speculated it was another kitchen fire. The guy from Channel 7 (their studio is right there) came out and tried see if there was a story.

At last they let us all back in. We lined up obediently to wait for the elevators. A lot of the kids took the stairs. A small group took cuts. Atticus told us later they are from the Arab Emirates, royalty, and don't ever stand in line. Hmm.

Another half hour went by and we finally found ourselves with our last load at the car.

It became apparent that this final load was not going to fit.

"It will fit if there is only a driver," Jeff said.

So we gave Atticus a train pass, Jeff went back to work, and I drove the loaded car home by myself.

Which is how I managed to come home from my first time of moving my kid out of the dorm without one key element—my kid.

Ann on the other hand did just fine and even managed to buy some kitchen stuff for next year. She of course made it sound easy. Which I am quite sure it was not.

COLLEGE VISITS

It is official, child number two, Grace, has decided to attend Valparaiso University. She will be studying Choral Music Education so she can be a high school choir teacher.

Now to get in to a good Music Education program you have to audition—as in sing opera-y type songs in Italian and German and stuff. Luckily, Grace actually knows how to do that but I have to admit, until this year, I had NO idea our choir teachers were so gifted.

Anyhoo, now that she knows where she's going my fun has ended for a while because I don't get to do any college visits until Lilly goes in 2015 and frankly, she's so sick of being dragged along to some of the visits, she is threatening not to go to college.

Which would be a shame because it turns out, I really, really liked the college visits. What's not to like about a road-trip with one (or more) of your kids who are at an age when you barely see them let alone TALK to them? I loved it all and consider it a perk of parenting.

Between March of 2011 and February 2013, first with Atticus, next with Grace, I visited more than a dozen colleges. Some of those were quick, informal drive-bys, but most were official visits. And since I am the only one in the family who went on ALL those trips, I am kind of the expert here.

Which makes me qualified to write one of my "what to expect" essays. So here goes:

Nail down a date for the visit: Good luck with this one. I am not sure there is anyone on earth busier than a high-school Junior unless that is a high-school Senior. But sometime between dances, concerts, school plays, exams, practices, and lessons you might find a day or two for a college visit. If you have to pull your kid from school to do this, surely the teachers will understand and be sympathetic, right? Wrong. They do not care why your student is missing school, they just hate it and will try to make your stressed out kid a little more stressed out.

This means you will make several of the college visits in the summer. Sounds nice but of course, who knows what a school really looks like without students? So you will probably end up having to come back during the year anyway. At least that will only be for the one or two schools that make the final cut.

Ask your student to register for a visit: If you have a slacker-child, skip this step and do it yourself. Really. If you have a responsible kid, this is not a big deal. I am speaking from experience.

Fly or drive to your destination and spend the night there so you will have plenty of time in the morning to get to find the Admissions Office: No matter how many times you do this, no matter how early you leave your hotel (or your home) no matter how many maps you have printed from the internet, you will somehow still be late for your campus tour.

Except for the final visit when you FINALLY realize you not only have to get near the campus you have to drive around it repeatedly the night before until you are sure you can re-create the route in the morning.

If you are traveling from home do not try to make up any lost time by speeding on the Tollway because you will get a ticket and then your child will really panic as she is being made late for her singing audition while the nice officer writes out your ticket and you will lose a day of your life when you have to go to the Daley Center to traffic court to get your license back. I mean, not that it happened to me, but it could.

Show up late for the campus tour: You would think it is not a big deal to be 10 to 15 minutes late for a campus tour. As a margin of error, it seems quite small when you consider the 24 or more hours you spent trying to get there. But It kind of is a big deal. Especially for your non-slacker child who hates to be late for anything.

Your slacker will shrug it off and even laugh as you run back and forth between the parking structure and wherever it is they make you go to get the parking voucher (this is never the same in any of the schools and it's not clear at all when it matters or not and when you might get ticketed or towed but you will be a little paranoid if you went to school in Ann Arbor where ticketing and towing visitors is a municipal sport.)

Join the group wherever they may be: Sometimes they are still milling around over the coffee and donuts and sometimes they are already in the middle of the quad. No worries, you really can't miss a crowd of adorable (if anxious) high school kids, their dumpy (and soon to be poor) parents, led by an overly-eager college kid dressed in school colors and talking animatedly while walking backwards.

Take the tour: You will see lots and lots of buildings (which don't really tell you much about the quality of education do they?) and one sample dorm room (most of which are pretty much the same as when you went to school), and be invited to eat in the cafeteria (that is not exactly fine dining but is SO much better than where you ate during your college years that you will start to get resentful) and the fitness center (ditto).

Ask your questions: You will get surprisingly candid answers sometimes even though you are asking people who are supposed to be selling their school. My two favorites were the weary financial advisor at one small conservatory-type college in Ohio who pretty much told us there was no money for our kids unless they were quite poor, and the K-College professor of photography who more or less said there was no reason he knew of why someone would want to pursue a career in photography. In both cases, I am fairly certain these gentlemen had smoked something semi-legal before meeting with us.

Feel nostalgic and resentful: You are only human if being on campus (your own or anyone else's) brings back vivid and fond memories of your years at the old ivy-covered alma mater. However, you will quickly remember too that nearly every vivid memory involves boys or alcohol or both. Even if the boy in your memory is now the father of the very child you are with, resist the temptation to share ANY of those stories. The last person on the face of the earth who wants to hear about your college escapades is your own child (or perhaps your mother). So zip it and share it later with your hubby.

And finally, let the bitterness go: You may feel some regret or resentment that your child actually has a plethora of colleges to choose from. Some of which look like a whole lot more fun or a better fit than where you went. Let this go. It was the 70s and no one was taking college visits (unless you were a Kennedy). Most of my peers have shared that their first "college visit" was something called "freshmen orientation." And we all turned out just fine.

If you have the privilege of taking a child to college visits, I hope you have as much fun as we have. And remember, don't speed on the Tollway, and don't talk about that game of quarters at Dooley's and you'll do just fine.

TURNABOUT AND THE PHOTO SHOOT

Saturday Lilly went to the Turnabout Dance in Glenview. That is the dance where the girls ask the boys. We called it Sadie Hawkins where I grew up but it's just another reason to have a formal dance and that's all good.

There are a lot of customs and rituals to follow for THE BIG DANCE and I realized that between our three kids and all the high school dances this was the 13th time around for Jeff and me which one might think makes us kind of experts.

I will share how things usually go from the parents' point of view.

1. For weeks before the big dance there will be much drama about who asked whom and who said yes and how the boy was asked. If you have a girl you will hear about this ad nauseam until your ears bleed. If you have a boy you will not even know there is a dance until just a few days before when he announces he needs a sport coat and a corsage.

2. There will be more drama as your girl searches for the perfect dress, shoes, and hairstyle. If you have a boy there will be much drama as you try to drag his dis-interested ass to the store and get him to try on a sport coat.

If you are lucky, your girl will agree to wear a dress already in the house from previous events or siblings. Just make sure the dress still fits, as in covers all her parts sufficiently. Trust me on this one — this is a mistake anyone can make — even if this is not their first time around.

3. For Turnabout the girls do the planning. Actually, they do the planning for all the dances. If done properly, this will involve restaurant reservations and spreadsheets to figure out who is driving whom (or a party bus ordered).

A wise mom (Carrie O) advised me early on NOT to get involved in any of this process. A bossy girl always takes care of this.

This is excellent advice. Just make sure your daughter did not volunteer to organize rides but did not actually do that and you don't find out until the picture-taking when a mom asks you for the driving schedule that your daughter did (but didn't really). Trust me, this could happen to anyone, even if they've done this a few times.

4. Picture-taking: This is where you go to someone's house or a public venue (like the Park District lobby) so you can take pictures of the 20 or so kids in your kid's group. You will only know one or two of the kids and one or two of the parents.

There is a lot of energy as everyone is anxious, looking around to see if they are properly dressed, and hoping to fit in. The kids are a little nervous too.

You will take a picture of your kid and his/her date as they try to figure out how to put a wrist corsage on or worse pin one on a lapel. Mom will end up pinning the corsage.

If you are lucky, the mother hosting the picture-taking assumes the role of assembling the kids for pictures. If you are unlucky no one will assume this roll and you will stand around a lot until a bossy girl takes over.

If you are really unlucky, the mom-host will see the entire evening as a photo-shoot followed by that annoying dinner and dance. After about 20 minutes of this nonsense (we remember one in particular where the girls were asked to jump up and down, now dance crazy, now put your hands like a train...you get the idea) feel free to leave.

You will take several pictures of your kid and his/her date as they stand awkwardly together because most of them go as "just friends".

Then you are obliged to take a group shot of all the girls. This takes forever as they come up with ridiculous formations to show off their finery.

Finally someone will have all the kids line up.

At some point you will take a picture or two of the boys altogether. Or not.

You will post one or two of these on Facebook. The rest you will delete.

5. And finally: You and your husband will go for a much-deserved cocktail and discuss how grown up the girls looked and how lost the boys looked. You will note which girl was dressed most inappropriately—as in not proper coverage—and hopefully it will not be your own daughter. But I am not saying that will always be the case, even if you are a veteran.

So that's pretty much how it goes. And even when you think you sort of understand how it goes, things can go awry. Which is true of all great parenting ventures so why would this be any different?

If you got to be a part of this fun ritual last week, I hope you had as much fun as we did. The kids? Oh yeah, I think they had fun too.

SPARE KEYS and CAPS AND GOWNS

I know I have written about this before but that just makes it even sillier that we pretty much re-lived the craziness.

I am talking about the first day back at school/work after Winter Break. It's amazing that it can look even more chaotic and disorganized than the official first day of school.

Here's how ours looked.

It actually started out with some planning and forethought. Sunday night, anticipating a crazy morning, I had the kids move the cars around in the driveway. We have three cars that we have to stack in a small driveway because 1) we do not use the tiny garage except to store junk and 2)even though we no longer have snow in Chicago, we are not allowed to park on the street from November to April in anticipation of the snow-plow needing to get through.

So Grace and Atticus went out and moved the cars in the order in which they would be driven out.
Jeff would be leaving his car for me because both Atticus and I had doctors' appointments at the same time on Monday.

In the morning I offered to drive Jeff to the train thinking it was the least I could do when he was giving up his car. Unfortunately, when the moment came to drive him (with the usual amount of spare time being 0 minutes), we could not find the key to my car. And the fun began.

We tore through my locker, my purse, my coat pockets and then I roared "Lilly wake your brother up and tell him to find my G*#Damned keys!" In the ensuing madness, I found my car key—Atticus had left it in HIS car. WTF How do you leave one car key in a different car of all places?

I went back in the house to find Atticus (who is home from college on winter break) wandering around in a just-woken-up-daze wearing only his boxers pretending to look for my keys.

"I found them in your car!" I said through gritted teeth "But can you all please just put the damn keys back where they go?!" Jeff stuck his head in the door at this moment to yell, "I'm going to miss my train!" And off we roared.

He made his train but barely. I came back to the house to find the girls trying to sneak out to school without having to listen to me rant again.

Later, when I found my spare key in my purse, I decided that perhaps it wasn't ALL the kids' fault. Jeff told me to resist the temptation to confess but I felt bad that I was really more a part of the problem than I had thought.

And when I went to my doctor's appointment and was told I was there on the wrong day, I had the sneaking suspicion that perhaps I am not just part of the problem but I am the problem.

And I thought that again this morning when Grace called from school to tell me it was cap and gown/grad announcement order day and everyone but her had a filled out form and I realized I not only did not have the form but had mistakenly thrown it away a few weeks ago thinking it was just an order for a class ring.

On the plus side, the kids have dutifully hung up the keys in their appointed space for two whole days now.

So if your first full work/school week of 2013 got off to a rocky start, rest assured, it did too for the Self-Righteous Housewife. And if past is any predictor of future it will next year too.

HAPPY NEW YEAR!

TWO BUTTONS DOWN, TWO TO GO

Most of you know I just dropped number one child off for college and may even be expecting me to write something sentimental and insightful about that experience but all I can say is man that sucks.

And if you are struggling with it like I am you might want to read my friend Christie Mellor's latest book, Fun Without Dick and Jane which is so very cleverly titled you just know it is full of helpful coping advice, which it is.

Instead, I want to write about how much I love back to school time and especially the clothes we wear for the occasion. I have loved back to school since I was in grade school and I would wear a plaid dress with a big white collar (had to be plaid, my favorite; had to be a dress, we were not allowed to wear pants to school back then). I love my first day of school photos with my gap-toothed grin as I stand clutching my pencil box. Remember those?

As far as I remember I wore the same version of that first plaid dress up until about junior high. I clearly remember my 7th grade outfit. By then we were allowed to wear pants to school and I wore purple bell-bottoms with laces on the side. I had a matching purple body suit (snapped at the crotch) that laced up the front and even though it was all one piece it was supposed to look like you were wearing a short-sleeved shirt over a long sleeved shirt which was the height of fashion in 1973. The bells on my purple pants were so wide they covered my shoes. That is how we measured if they were big enough. I could make a joke about that outfit but I think it speaks for itself.

And I loved going off to college in Ann Arbor with my THREE Pendleton wool skirts my mom made me especially the red and black plaid one. They looked fabulous with my shetland sweaters and my penny-loafers which were back in style in the late 70s after having been mothballed since the 50s.

Since I have had my kids I wear my own red and plaid skirt every first day of school when I get my picture taken with the kids—see above. I have worn that skirt for the past 14 years.

Except.

Except that this year, I had to unbutton not one but TWO of the buttons on my skirt to fit in it. I know, I could buy a new one but really, I am much too old to wear a plaid skirt to begin with let alone buy a new one.

Several years back, Barbara Brotman of the Chicago Tribune wrote a whole column on being too old to wear a plaid pleated skirt which I literally read while wearing my plaid pleated skirt. I am sorry to say I cannot find that column and if any of you do, let me know (Maria?).

Anyhoo, I pointed out to Lilly that I had two buttons unbuttoned and that maybe it was time to give up on the skirt but she loves tradition more than any of us and looked at me with horror at the suggestion. I guess I have two more buttons to go so I don't see any reason to get rid of it now.

And by the way, speaking of tradition, I did get to read "Kissing Hand" to all the kids even Atticus on the day we drove him to college but I had to sneak in his room and read it to him while he was barely awake so he wouldn't hear me cry and I also had to change some of the words to nonsense like, "Chester skipped off to school and did not look back the little bastard," also so I would not cry too hard.

So, if you have any back to school memories of particularly fetching or ridiculous clothes you wore or wear still, let me know.

DON'T LET THE DOOR HIT YOU

Well here we are. August 1st and that means tuition bills are due and (for many of us) our eldest child is getting ready to go to college for the first time.

I feel like we've prepared for this for a long, long time. We watched our friends do it, we've listened to their advice and now it's our turn.

So far they have been right: This is a difficult, sad, often grief-filled time in which you struggle to deal with the impending separation—but most of the time you will be thinking—hey can you get out of my house now?

Yes, just as I was counseled by the wise women who have gone before me, a young person between his or her senior year of high school and first year of college is umm, well, kind of a pain in the neck. This is nature's way of making it easier to say goodbye.

I'm not sure what it is a mom might find annoying...Maybe it's the way he sleeps until noon then spends the early evening hours with his girlfriend and the late nights on the computer until the wee hours. Could it be his general attitude that he no longer has any family obligations but is still entitled to the whole free food/free laundry thing? Or the way he leaves his socks on the kitchen floor and sometimes his pants and shirt too when he comes home hours after you have already been in bed. Perhaps it's that he's taken to showering in your shower (it's closer than his) so when you go to shower there are no clean towels.

It's true, I will cry when I leave him at the dorm but he's virtually already gone. I only see the back of his head as he plays on the computer or leaves the house yet again to "hang" with someone.

His sisters and I have taken to talking about him as if he's gone. "Hey, can I put my bunnies in Atticus's room now?" one asks. "I'm still here!" he cries indignantly.

The other sister (and I) can't wait to clear out the hovel in the corner of the kitchen that has been his computer/work space. We pour over Houzz online and pick out new furniture to fill in the space. (That corner below...what do you think?)

I remember when my mom went to parent orientation at Michigan State for my sister (the eldest) and came back and said, "They told us not to turn their bedrooms into sewing rooms. They need to know they're welcome at home." So at first I said no to the bunny hutch idea. But then a wise friend suggested, "Why don't you just move the rabbits back out when he comes home? You can enjoy the extra space while he's away."

Good idea.

So we're all a bit sad that Atticus will be leaving soon (in twenty-four days, three hours, and six minutes).

But we're also looking forward to an actual kitchen table, a sock-free floor, and clean dry towels.

(A special shout out to Kelly and Wendy who have been there from kindergarten...can you believe it's really happening?)

ARTISTS IN TRAINING

When Grace was first born and Atticus was just 19 months old we moved to a high-rise in the city on Wacker Drive. We had a view of the lake and Grant Park and rode the elevator with a former and a future governor (Edgar and Ryan). It was the summer of the OJ trial and it was so hot people were dying left and right in the city. Fireworks were shot out every night over the newly renovated Navy Pier and we could see them and hear them from the kids' bedroom.

Every day the kids and I would head out to explore with the double-stroller. I quickly got to know the underground pedway system (to escape the heat) and soon walked off the baby weight and then some. Sometimes I would push them down to the Art Institute (the stroller entrance is in the back on Columbus—can't get in on the lion side) where we've always had a membership.

Sometimes I just nursed Grace in the family area while Atticus looked at art books. Other times we would wander around and stop to people watch. I like to look at people looking at art more than I like to look at art really. Most days we sat in the room with Monet's haystacks and enjoyed the cool, quiet room and then went on to get a snack. After we moved out to Glenview I still took them in to the city whenever I could and we almost always included a brief stop at the museum. That might be the best part about having a museum pass—that you can pop in for a short time and not feel obligated to look at everything all at once—which is really just a chore.

During these visits we had some memorable moments like the time Grace petted the horse on a Remington statue. Atticus and I had a heart-attack—the guard never noticed. To this day she says, "Well how was I supposed to know you're not supposed to touch it?" Or the time Grace tripped and nearly went through the Chagall windows.

Sometimes we would see young adults in the galleries, dressed funky, sketching the art, or taking notes, or just discussing the art with each other. Art students I would think—how cool is that? I was vaguely aware that the Art Institute also has a school attached to it but did not give it much thought.

So it is a great surprise to me that after the long hard college search it turns out that is where Atticus will be going—the School of the Art Institute of Chicago. During all those visits it NEVER occurred to me that one of the kids might go to school there one day.

He will be studying photography and print-making starting next fall. And one thing's for sure, he will feel quite at home there. More on the School of the Art Institute of Chicago in my next post...

MORE ABOUT THE SCHOOL OF THE ART INSTITUTE

I never really thought of Atticus as artistic. He is not the kid who worked feverishly on art projects or brought home stuff from art class—that would be Grace.

But he started taking photography classes as a Freshman and never really stopped. Still, I didn't think of it as an artistic pursuit but more of an interest of his because he is, after all, a serial interest taker.

Last spring I finally noticed he was doing more with his photography. One day he asked to use a speaker from the computer and he stretched a black balloon over it, poured paint on it, then turned on music.

When the paint jumped up he took pictures (see left).

And on vacation in Maine while the other kids ran around the grounds he covered his bedroom windows in black garbage bags and created a room-sized camera (see left above).

Still I just thought it was just a hobby of his so I was surprised when he declared he wanted to study photography in college. And surprised when the Art Institute sent someone out to the high school to help the kids with their portfolios that the woman told him his stuff was fabulous and he should apply to their school. And shocked when he not only got accepted but was offered an amazing scholarship based on his portfolio.

So that's a quick version of how he got to the SAIC. As promised in my previous post, here's some more info on the school that is kind of cool and we have learned since he was accepted.

• The school came before the museum. In the 1860s some artists started a school of art. Their personal collections of art became the start of the museum

• The Chicago Art Institute is the third largest art museum in the world: after the Louvre and the Met

• As a student you have access to all the art in the museum. Only about 25% of the collection is out at any time. You can go into the archives and say "I'd like to look at Picasso's diaries" and they'll hand you white gloves and let you have at it.

• There are dorms. They are high-rise loft apartments in the Theatre District. Every student has a drafting table in their room. The entire 17th floor is an art studio open 24/7. When Atticus heard about the drafting tables he was sold.

So next time you are in Chicago, don't forget to visit our museum and keep your eyes peeled. That artsy kid prowling the galleries just might be mine.

LIMPING TOWARD COLLEGE

As many of you know, the first wave of college application deadlines is coming up on November 1. I thought this might be a good time to recap the whole process (from a parent's point of view) up until this point. Here's how it has looked so far:

Last winter: Start worrying about campus visits. Don't actually do anything about it but talk to every mom you know until you hear a rational strategy that you might follow. Hear this advice "Don't take any special trips out of the way, but visit colleges if you are traveling anyway." Love this advice! Take this advice and run with it.

Spring Break: While in Florida go ahead and visit a Florida college:University of Miami. As you are escorted around the lush green grounds taking in the sights of bikini-top girls and frisbee-playing boys wonder why in the hell you chose to go to a frigid Big-Ten school that had weather like this ummm, well, NEVER. Fall into a deep depression as you realize that your fun college days (which were definitely not as fun as these kids are having...hey are those hammocks between palm trees over there?) are not only behind you but decades behind you. Try not to cry just a little as you are filled with deep, bitter, regret. Have your kid declare this school is NOT his cup of tea.

Summer: Make a few half-assed plans to travel to see more colleges. Try not to listen to your friends when they tell you they have been flying along the East and West Coasts taking their smarty-pants kid to colleges. Wonder why you are even friends with such over-achievers. Make a note to start having coffee and drinks with people who have much lower aspirations for their offspring. Visit some of the schools you can get to easily. Repeat more or less the Florida experience ("Why didn't I come here?! This is way more fun/cool/funky/ than where I went?") Have kid declare the most expensive one you visit "Is just where I belong". Wonder how people pay for this. Get used to everyone in the world asking your kid what his college plans are. Coach him to just say the name of a college so they will stop bugging him. Maybe even make up a name of a college to watch people make a funny frowny face as they try to think of something to say.

Late Summer: Realize you are in no way going to find "the school" for your kid before application time. The one school he declared he belongs at does not offer the program he wants. Realize further you don't have to figure this out right now...he can apply and then you can visit the ones he gets into. See his transcripts and realize that when the counselors talked about the importance not of just the grades but the trend of the grades that his are not trending the right way. Realize maybe you won't have many schools to visit when it all shakes out.

Fall: Start full-time nagging of your kid regarding application process. Attend yet another parent meeting to go over all the things your slacker kid is supposed to do to apply to each college. Curl up in the fetal position just thinking about it. Watch as your kid acts like it is no big deal. Continue nagging. Set up a weekly meeting with him to go over the progress he has not made and continue to nag. You should be nagging him about filling out the common application, writing an essay, getting teacher recommendations, sending ACT scores, and ordering transcripts. Nag some more.

Early October: It is crunch time. Go out to dinner with your husband and talk about nothing but how your kid has not done anything towards applying to college. Realize, hey, I went to college. Call the blockhead into the living room for the weekly ass-kicking and inform him it is up to HIM to get himself into a college—you are done. Watch his face with its funny mixture of relief and horror.

Mid October: Watch your kid scramble to get all the things done he needs to get done. Enjoy this tiny moment in which you have managed to put the stress back where it belongs. Mix a cocktail even as he sweats over his essay. Be very happy you do not have to do this. Be a little sad you do not get a do-over for college.

So that's where we are. How about you? For all of you with Seniors (and I know a lot of you) I hope it's going pretty much on target and your kids make the November 1 deadline. If you have had to nag them a tiny bit...I'm pretty sure you are not alone.

Happy Halloween!

THE ACTs

A short time ago both my high-schoolers took the ACTs. For my European readers, this is a general college admissions test kids take primarily in the midwest. East and west coast require a similar test called the SATs.

Anyhoo, Grace, a junior was taking it for the first time just to see how she would do and Atticus, a senior, was taking it for the second time to see if he could bump his score a point or two which can translate into scholarship money.

The test was at 8 a.m. on a Saturday and I nudged Jeff early and suggested we go downstairs and offer to make them breakfast before they go.

When we got to the kitchen we found the following scene:

Grace was standing at the kitchen table fully dressed. She declined the offer of breakfast—she had already made herself a smoothie and an omelet and put her dishes in the dishwasher. Her calculator was out along with four spare batteries, neatly arranged next to several sharpened pencils, and her test admission ticket. She was making herself a healthy snack to have during the test break and going over the directions she had printed out one last time.

Atticus was sitting at the computer clad only in his boxer shorts. He had headphones on and was chuckling over his on-line morning cartoons. He declined the offer of breakfast because he was already eating a muffin, much of which was falling apart in crumbs down his bare belly.

There was nothing regarding the test in sight...not even a number two pencil.

None of this was a surprise of course but it is hard not get a little panicky when you see someone not even dressed, 45 minutes before a big test. So I felt I should speak up.

Me: "Don't you want to print out an admission ticket like your sister's?"
Atticus: "Oh. Do I need that?"

Sigh. Yes, 19 months apart and it's like they're from different planets. Just when you think maybe you had something to do with your children (for better or worse) you come across a scenario like this and realize they could have been raised by wolves and Grace would still be the kind of person who has spare batteries for her calculator and Atticus might even forget to take the test (oh yeah, he DID forget to take the SAT he was signed up for last June).

So parents, remind yourself today if you are gloating over your over-achiever or fretting over your under-achiever, you probably had nothing to do with it anyway.

AU REVOIR!

The local high school has been hosting some French students the last few weeks and I seem to hear about them all the time. The local paper did a feature on them; both Atticus and Grace have met them all since they came to speak to their French classes; and Lilly's friend Carolyn's family is hosting one of them. That's some of them in the photo wearing sunglasses they received as a gift from the American students.

It seems everyone loves them. They are beautiful and they speak with that most coveted of all accents. Lilly gets updates from Carolyn about the student they are hosting. His name is Tristan and here are the stories she's collected so far:

On day 1 when he woke up after sleeping off his jet-lag for hours, Carolyn asked if he would like something to drink. Tristan responded, "No thank you, I do not thirst."

Day 3: he discovered Eggo Waffles and now each morning he asks for them.

Day 4: his host mom asked if he'd like to drive the car and he said yes. She asked if he were scared and he said yes.

Day 5: when asked if he wanted more Eggo Waffles he said, "No thank you. My stomach is already crowded."

So when Atticus and Grace brought a note home from their French teacher asking if we'd be willing to host a French student who may be stranded by the volcanic ash incident (a different group than the Glenview group—these kids have been in Ohio but are scheduled to fly out of O'Hare tomorrow) we raised our hands enthusiastically and said "OUI".

Cute French kids that say hilarious things like "my stomach is crowded". Heck yes, sign us up.

Unfortunately for us, with the planes flying again it looks like we won't get one after all. In fact, even if they are stranded we may not get one because it turns out that we were just one of 40 families who raised their hands and said "OUI" and there are only 9 students who might need to be housed.

And you gotta love that. I'm quite certain that all over the US there are families opening their doors to stranded exchange students and the same thing is happening in Europe to stranded American students.

So despite the lost commerce of last week's volcanic episode you gotta love the whole thing: that we were reminded that yes indeed, Europe is very, very far away and hard to get to without planes; that it isn't just terrorist attacks that ground planes but mother nature too; that when people are displaced and need a place to stay there are always friendly families willing to open their doors and just say "Bonjour, may I get you an Eggo Waffle?"

FIRST DAY OF FIRST GRADE

It's been five years since I wrote this. To all the moms saying goodbye to first-graders and college freshman in particular—here's to you!

My youngest started first grade today and all week long everyone I run into says, "What will you do with your free time now?" A lot of people ask this in jest, knowing full well there isn't much you can do with the few hours when all the kids are out of the house at once. Others ask in earnest knowing that a world of possibilities has just opened up.

I have some ideas. I'm going to start exercising again. I'm going to write more. I'm going to finish my novel. Some of my friends will go back to work with the help of sitters and nannies. Others will fill up the time doing more around the house, taking part-time jobs, or volunteering even more of their time to the schools. It is strange but as a stay-at-home mom if you do your job really well you are rewarded by having your job taken away from you little by little. Today I was demoted to part-time. It's not a huge chunk of time; 9:00 to 2:30 due to staggered start times among my three children, but nevertheless it's a much bigger chunk of time than I've had in eleven years.

It's not a total shock of course. The free-time comes quite gradually really, from the crazed frenzied days of breast-feeding and diaper-changing to the slightly less frantic days of potty-training and pre-school schedules to the relative calm of kindergarten and early elementary days. But some parts of it are not so gradual. Like today, the first day of school. It's a wrenching change in my life. My youngest is the best of my three children at expressing herself. This makes parenting her sometimes easier and sometimes much more challenging. Last night, she sat in my lap as I read "The Kissing Hand" and as I struggled to get through that tear-jerker she interrupted me to say, "Mama, I am not ready for first grade." "What do you mean?" I asked prepared to give her a pep-talk, to remind her that her best friend is in her class, she has the same bus route as last year, and she can already read chapter books. "I'm not ready to be away from you for so many hours," she said simply.

This stopped me dead in my tracks because the truth is I'm not really ready to be away from her for so many hours either. I mean maybe more than the 2 ½ hours of a kindergarten day but I really don't need her to be gone from me more than seven hours which is what it turns out to be with the bus ride to and from school. Can't they have a four hour day in first grade while we all adjust? My eyes filled with tears but I turned my head so she could not see. I forced a cheerful answer, "But honey, you were gone that many hours just yesterday with Margaret when you went to her house and then to the movies and you didn't mind that." "But I can't be away from you that many hours every day," she countered.

Now I began to cry in earnest, thankful that children seldom look their moms in the eye and as I sat with her in my lap trying to compose myself and most unhelpfully I remembered a Dave Barry column in which he drives his son Rob to Kindergarten for the first time and as they sit in the car outside the school, saying goodbye, Rob asks, "Daddy, how long do I have to do this?" and he can't bring himself to answer, but he thinks, "Forever and ever." I remember crying when I read that column and I didn't even have children then. I shook my head trying to get the image of Rob and Dave Barry out of my head and to distract myself I tried to figure out how old Rob must be now. He's probably in college or older, and not nearly as close to his father as he was when he was five. That was no help so I lifted Lilly off my lap and told her I'd be right back. I went into the bathroom and closed the door and sobbed into a bathroom towel. I was thinking of all the other mothers in my town, in my state, and probably in the world doing the same thing; crying into a bathroom towel because who else can you cry to? If only we had some acceptable way to share our collective grief maybe it would help but parenthood demands we act cheerful and even relieved when our little ones begin to leave the nest. For the most part we are relieved. But we are grieving too.

So please remember that when you see us looking a little dazed at the bus stop in the morning or a little anxious for the bus in the afternoon. Do not be deceived by our breezy answers to your question, "What will you do with your day now that the kids are all in school?" Because we're not really sure ourselves. Oh we have lots of ideas; but we are afraid that any them will pale in comparison to the wondrous job we are leaving behind, the privilege of caring for a little one 24/7.

CENSORSHIP

Grace tried out for the talent show at her high school this week. They were required to sing a passage from *Don't Stop Believin* that old chestnut by Journey which seems to be resurrected every few years by politicians, sports teams, and this year our new favorite show, *Glee*. They gave her a copy of the sheet music to practice and Lilly was looking it over when she said, "Hey, they cut out the line that says 'smell of wine and cheap perfume'. It just says 'smell of cheap perfume'." We all puzzled over this odd bit of editing. It was clear the word "wine" had been whited-out (is that the past-tense of white-out?). Grace worked on the music a while trying to figure out how you even sing the song without enough syllables.

The next day in glee club Grace's teacher mentioned it. "I cut out the w-i-n-e word," she said spelling it out as if it were a curse word.

Is wine a bad word now? This is the same school that just put on *To Kill a Mockingbird* and wisely kept the "n" word. What the fuh? The "n" word stays but the "w" word goes? I didn't even know it was the "w" word. What would this teacher think if she knew I sometimes have a glass of "w" right in front of my children!

The puzzling thing is that this appears to be the decision of a single teacher. It's not like the school has a "no singing songs with alcohol in them" policy (well, I don't *think* they do). Though if they did you might wonder how they would sing a lot of songs like *Days of "w" and Roses* or Bob Marley's *Red Red "w"*. (A side note, *The Days of Wine and Roses* was the prom theme when my sister was a high school senior, which was only slightly more inappropriate than my prom theme which was *Nights in White Satin* which kind of makes you wonder where the adult supervision was in our school but then again that's what we get for electing a burnout as our class president that year.)

Anyhoo back to the censorship at hand: for some reason this teacher took it upon herself to edit the song. I don't know why. There are no banned books at my kids' school and this spring they are going to put on the play *Rent*. I hope this teacher doesn't get her hands on that script because instead of the play being about a bunch of gay people battling AIDS she might change it to a bunch of heterosexuals who all contract really bad cases of mono from kissing.

I'm kind of perplexed by this "w" thing. Would it be appropriate for me to protest to the school about censoring music? On the one hand it is a song by Journey and I'm not sure they've exactly earned the right to artistic freedom. On the other hand, if we let this go what's to stop it from escalating? I can only imagine the Holiday Concert in which *Holly Jolly Christmas* would have a line that says "and have a cup of cocoa" or the line from *Baby It's Cold Outside* (which my kids call the creepiest date rape song of all time — and it really is if you listen to the words) could be "hey what's in this milk?"

I was mulling over the right to free speech and my duty as a bleeding heart liberal in all of this when Grace told me a story that made me realize I did not need to intervene. It seems that during the audition process one of the seniors sang the song his own way in protest. He got a big laugh when he sang, "Smell of fermented grape juice and cheap perfume," and I have to hand it to him because really, one of the most effective tools against censorship has to be a good dose of teen-aged ridicule.

Don't stop believin'.

Photo Interlude

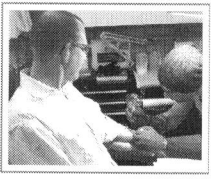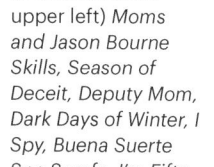
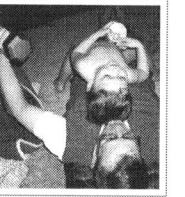

(Clockwise from upper left) *Moms and Jason Bourne Skills, Season of Deceit, Deputy Mom, Dark Days of Winter, I Spy, Buena Suerte Spa Serafa, I'm Fifty, Are You a Good Parent?, I Remember You, Mindful Neglectful, Your Someday Tattoo*

(Clockwise from upper left) *47, 48, 49 Oblivion, Prenatal to Prom, Confirming I'm An Idiot, As the Nest Empties, Shopping for Big Brother, Teenage Boys, Delightful, 8th Grade Graduation, Prom, Upside Down Duck*

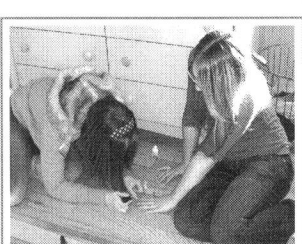

(Clockwise from upper left) *Moving Out of the Dorm, Turnabout and the Photoshoot, Spare Keys and Caps and Gowns, More About the School of the Art Institute (two Atticus art photos), Au Revoir!, First Day of First Grade, Limping Toward College, High School Has Changed*

(Clockwise from upper left) *Glazed Ham, The Christmas Party, Halloween: Then and Now, What Would Tyra Do?, The Arnold Story, The Zoo, Friends' Parents and Parents' Friends, It's All Relative*

(Clockwise from upper left) *Texting 1-2-3, Crushes, I Wanna Hold Your Hand, Smile For the Camera, My Dog Tells You About the Skunk, Beauty and Short Hair, Be Kind on Thursday, Free the Presidential Apostrophe*

(Clockwise from upper left) *That Drawer and Band Polos, Love Notes in Lunch Bags, Out of the Woods, Lilly Look Back, Casseroles Cure Cancer, Stranger Angels, To Sleep Perchance to Dream, Afterword*

HIGH SCHOOL HAS CHANGED IN 30 YEARS

Now that I have two kids in high school I'm pretty much an expert on the topic. Especially since I have both a boy and a girl there. Yes, two is definitely a statistically significant number when n is 2 and N is a bazillion. I learned that in statistics.

Anyhoo, here are a few observations in case you do not have a high schooler in your life and you would like to be in the know or a real "hep cat".

1. First of all, **no one says real hep cat**. I'm not sure anyone ever did.

2. **Hugging**: hugging is very big in high school. Girls hug boys, boys hug boys, but most of all girls hug girls. They hug good morning and good bye. They hug when they run into each other in stores. They hug because they can. We never hugged. We only hugged people we were dating or when we said goodbye to friends at the end of the summer. No, not even then. We were repressed and more than a little homo-phobic. They are not. They are like Europeans or something—all this touching and hand-holding and cheek-kissing. I think this is a great development because it's healthy to hug and be hugged. Yet in our culture after hugging, snuggling and petting our kids like kittens for the first 10 years of their life we drop them like lepers when they hit puberty. No wonder they're in need of a hug! All this innocent

hugging they do, I would think, could even postpone the inevitable "advanced hugging" which is what kids who crave affection often get into.

3. **Dating:** no one goes out on a date. Not like we did. No one. I repeat, no one calls a girl on the house phone (yes, that's what they call that thing plugged into your kitchen wall) and says, "Hello Debbie, would you care to go to a movie with me on Friday?" (partly because no one is named Debbie anymore. What happened to all the Debbies?) No. High schoolers tend to travel in packs and then sort of peel off unofficially to do their he-ing and she-ing. So the dating looks more like a pack of antelope heading off to the watering hole. If anyone is "asking" anyone on a date, it will take place in the form of a text or a message on Facebook. "Do u wanna go to da movies?" which means dads can no longer terrorize potential suitors calling daughters and they will never have the chance to yell "Tell that kid not to honk his horn anymore," because kids don't honk their horns in the driveway anymore they text each other.

4. They are much, **much more connected** than we were: With the aid of texting and "social media" (that means Facebook and MySpace) the kids all know where everyone is at any moment. And what they are doing. All the time. That's why as you drive to grandma and grandpa's for Christmas you will know that Maggie is on her way to see her grandparents in Ohio and Sam is going out to the movies with a bunch of friends, and Michael is skiing in Colorado. I kind of like this too. Somehow it takes away a little of the sting of having to spend long periods of time with your own family (don't pretend you don't remember that feeling.)

5. **They are better friends** than we were: Yes, I have to say that despite my concern that all this electronic communicating would result in the death of verbal communication and the decline of western society in general it doesn't seem to be the case. In fact, the opposite seems to have occurred. With all this connecting it is even easier to check on a sick friend, help a friend who forgot her homework, plot to decorate a locker for a birthday, and make plans to watch a friend at a swim meet. These things just lend themselves to a casual text whereas several separate phone calls might be just enough of an obstacle to pass on the whole thing.

6. They **"joke" in electronic ways** and they are dang funny: Have you been "rick roll'd"? Well that's what happens when a friend sends you an email with a link that might say "check out this video it's so cool funny cats dancing." But when you click on it (and I hope you will) you get transferred to a YouTube video of Rick Astley singing "Never Gonna Give You Up" which is quite possibly the most atrocious, cheesy, music video ever made. They pass along YouTube videos and jokes just like your friends do but theirs tend to be a little more culturally relevant than those ladies from the 30's doing that freaky circus barn dance.

7. **Some things never change**: Even though a lot of things have changed a lot of things haven't. There are still burnouts, now called "emo", and jocks and cheerleaders and the usual assortment of nerds—drama, band, chess club. And even though a lot of the lingo has changed a lot of it hasn't. Just the other day the kids were discussing a girl in their school who dresses

inappropriately. Too short, too tight, too much. You get the idea. Atticus said, "We have a name for girls like that." I leaned in close, eager to hear the latest slang for "girls like that". "Really?" I asked, "What is it?" He knows I fancy myself a student of current slang and he knows he is one of the few translators that I have. So he grinned as he shared it with me, "Whore."

PART 04: ENTERTAINMENT

AUNT DELIA & THE CHRISTMAS PARTY

F amily legend has it that my Aunt Delia (the most beautiful and glamorous of the aunts) was known to host fun parties but when she was done with the party she would just leave and go to bed.

I do not know if this really happened or maybe happened once or many times but it is a good story.

We hosted our annual Christmas Party this past Saturday. This is a great bash with about forty of our best friends and neighbors in Glenview we have hosted for fifteen years.

At about 9:30 I was talking to someone and thought, "Oh my gosh, I'm not sure I can stay awake all night." I said, "Excuse me, I have to check on Lilly, " which is a preposterous statement as Lilly is fourteen and was sensibly holed up in her bedroom ignoring the noise below.

I went into my bedroom and emboldened by thoughts of Aunt Delia lay down on the bed. In a few minutes Jeff came up the stairs. I thought he came to check on me but he was surprised to find me there.

"I just need to lie down a minute," he said and did.

We lay there holding hands wondering how long we could be gone from our own party without being missed. We figured hours actually.

We listened to the roar from below and it was quite festive and comforting like when you were a kid and your parents had a party and you could hear it all. It was a little annoying when their bursts of laughter interrupted your *Partridge Family* but otherwise it was fun and reassuring.

All those voices talking and laughing were so lovely. I thought about all those friends downstairs who have been there for us over the years through the good times and most recently the challenging times and I thought about how much I love them all and I may have gotten a little weepy—in a good way.

After about fifteen minutes I rose, refreshed. "Come on," I said to Jeff.

"I love *martineesh*," Jeff declared. I suggested maybe he had enough martinis but he waved me off.

We went back and I was just fine, fully alert and ready for the rest of the party (and so was Jeff by the way—he took a walk around the block with his BFF Dan instead of having another martini) In fact, I made it all the way to 1:00 a.m. and I did not feel the urge to gather everyone's coats off the bed and hand them back to the few stragglers like I did in 2005 (or so). Nor did I have to put my pajamas on which is how I signal my dear friend Beth that it is time to go when she is visiting.

So next time you are at a party and need a little break go lie down. Even if if is your own party.

If anyone gives you a hard time about it, tell them Aunt Delia told you to.

Merry Christmas and Happy Holidays

THE TRUMP-INATOR

When I play the card game Euchre with my family (which is something we do nearly every time a bunch of Zimmermans are together) I have trouble keeping track of what trump is. This should not be difficult—there are only four choices—hearts, clubs, spades, and diamonds but I find myself frequently asking, "What's trump?" and hearing the standard reply of "Hearts, Maxine," accompanied by groans at my ridiculous inability to remember something so simple. "Hearts Maxine" is an expression my family uses because my cousin Maxine was sort of the pioneer of forgetful Euchre players and asked what trump was so many times that the phrase was coined.

As the next generation is learning to play Euchre, I find they are even more impatient with my forgetfulness than my own siblings so I have devised a way to keep track. I simply take out four number two cards (you only use 9-Aces in Euchre) and set them at my elbow. When trump is called I turn over the two of whatever suit was called and that way instead of having to ask all the time I can just glance down. This is such a brilliant idea that I have named my stack of four cards "The Trump-inator" Never mind that sometimes the Trump-inator gets tangled up in the discard pile or worse yet the score-keeping cards, it works pretty well overall.

I think The Trump-inator is so ingenious that I am starting to collect other ideas that need a similar solution—situations when people frequently have problems keeping track. Here are a few ideas. I don't actually have a device to solve these problems; I just think it would be cool if there were such a thing. Let me know if you have any ideas and no, "there's an app for that" is not an answer. I don't have a Smart Phone.

1. The Link-inator: this handy device would somehow collect all the websites, YouTube videos, shopping links, and family photos that are referenced in a given conversation and automatically send them to everyone involved. For example, you are out to dinner with your sister and you reference a slutty drunken picture of one of the cousins you saw on FaceBook and she says she hasn't seen it so you say you'll send her the link the next day but by the next morning you realize that you said that about several things and you cannot for the life of you remember what the links were that you thought were so damned funny/relevant/interesting the night before. This would solve the problem and ensure that your sister will never again miss that amazing video of a cat playing piano.

2. The dinner-party-guest-name-inator: This pocket-sized implement has the names of all the guests at the dinner party you are going to along with photos and dotted lines to show who is married to whom. This will eliminate the need for the conversation in the car on the way to the dinner party when your husband keeps saying, "Now what's Susan's husband's name? The Jackass?" and "Will that hot babe from book club be there—what's her name?"

3. The anti-re-gift-inator: This is a discrete stamp noting the date and giver on the bottom of every hostess gift and bottle of wine you receive so that you may never ever accidentally give that bottle of Prosecco back to the person who gave it to you.

4. What's-her-name-inator: Somehow this projects a person's name above her head at a social function so that you will never again know the panic you feel when you realize you need to introduce two people and have somehow managed to forget the name of the person you know best, perhaps someone you know very well and have known for years, I'm just saying, Coffee Friend 2, this could happen.

Just imagine how awesome the world would be if we had these wonderful little helpers. But for now, you can take comfort in knowing you'll never again have to ask what's trump, Maxine.

GLAZED HAM

My mother comes out from the kitchen and says to the room at large, "Who wants glaze on the ham?" Everyone's hand shoots up except my Grandmother who at 95 is understandably hard of hearing and fussing with her annoying hearing aid.

"What are you talking about?" she says to me as I am siting closest to her.

"Glazed ham!" I shout. She shakes her head no, she did not catch that. Now the room begins a ridiculous, yet all too familiar game of trying to get the hard of hearing person to hear you. My sister tries a little louder. "Glazed Ham!" My aunt tries, adding a bizarre hand gesture that presumably represents the drizzling of glaze on a ham. My children, lined up on the couch politely visiting with the adults are watching all of this are trying not to laugh but when Aunt Nancy adds the confusing hand gesture it is too much for them and they bust out laughing as does Jeff who is sitting with them.

"GLAZED HAM!" I shout. Grandma fusses with her hearing aid.

"It's talking to me," she says and I'm not sure what she means. Please lord, don't tell me she's hearing voices in her head. "It talks to me all the time. Tells me the batteries are going. Asks me about the settings I want."

"That's cool," I say.

She shakes her head no. "No it's not. I just want it to let me hear. Where's the button for that?"

My sister comes in from the kitchen with a note that says, "Mom wants to know if you want glaze on your ham." My grandmother reads it and registers a face that says, "Good lord is THAT all you were talking about?" She shrugs and says, "Sure."

This scene is familiar to me. As a child I was frequently in the room with an elderly relative with poor hearing. My paternal grandmother wore hearing aids for years and my great grandmother was stone deaf but wore the hearing aids in a futile attempt to hear something going on around her. I know all the tricks—speak clearly and directly. Try a different pitch rather than just talk louder. But even all of this does not always work.

My sister comments on how much this sucks. Why are hearing aids just never quite right? Unlike glasses, which seem to immediately correct the problem, I have never known anyone who popped those aids in their ears, looked around and said, "I can hear!" No, there is always the fussing and screeching and fumbling with batteries.

I already have a small amount of hearing loss—normal I assume for my age—but with the family history it is pretty much inevitable that some day I too will be staring blankly as my grandchildren shout "Glazed ham!" at me.

This will not be remotely fun for me but I hope at least it will be funny to my grandchildren. I know it is to my kids. This morning at the breakfast table I got a huge laugh from them all by just shouting, "Glazed ham!" Lilly added to the hilarity by imitating her aunt's hand gesture, the now accepted international sign for dribbling sugary syrup on a piece of pork.

Happy spring to you all. I hope you had a wonderfully glazed ham yourselves yesterday and I hope no one had to shout too much for you to hear them.

SUMMER HOLIDAYS

As most of you know, the last Saturday before school starts is the major North American holiday, known as "Molly-day the Holiday" (which is rather tricky to say as the words rhyme but not really—I think that is called assonance which I only know from that movie, Educating Rita. That was a good movie wasn't it?)

Anyhoo, if you don't know about this holiday, which was invented last year by Lilly and Grace, it is a day in which we spend the entire day celebrating our dog, Molly. You arise early and give her a special breakfast (the wet food she hardly ever has). Then you pull her back to bed and let her sleep in with you. Later you will take her to the park. In the wagon since she is the only dog in Glenview who really, really will not take a walk.

In the afternoon you might dress her up. Maybe in that dog Flamenco dress Aunt Beth helped you make (that's what she's wearing above). Then around 3:00 your friends with dogs come over with their dogs and you all run around the back yard and have a bona fide play date. After that, you will all come in the house (with gates placed strategically so mom won't lose her mind) and enjoy the dog cake you made out of kibble and peanut butter and the human cake Grace baked for the people guests.

In the evening you snuggle on the couch and watch (what else?) "Benji" and "Air Bud" and Molly's favorite, Animal Planet. And finally, you will go to bed where Molly will sleep right next to you. Oh, yes, well, she does that every night but tonight you will both be really tired from all the festivities of Molly-day the Holiday and your sleep will be especially delicious.

I hope you enjoy whatever it is your family does to celebrate this big day and remember, life is much too short to confine yourself to only the holidays on the calendar.

COUNTRY STRONG

Although we are brought up to believe that country music is something that only southerners listen to the real truth is that anytime you are more than 20 miles from a Starbucks and a Target (sure signs of urban civilization) and you turn on the radio, you will be inundated with music that appeals to your inner-hillbilly even if you are well north of the Mason-Dixon line.

I was reminded of this again as I made a family road trip a few weeks back and though I swear we never got farther south than Oberlin, Ohio the radio played a soundtrack that made it seem like we were deep in Deliverance-land. I kept a nervous eye peeled for a banjo-playing simpleton at every turn.

If you like to listen to the radio as you travel (as I do) to give yourself a break from your own playlist you have the following choices whenever you are out in Sarah Palin Land: 3 country stations, 1 oldies station, 1 to 3 right-wing Christian stations, and a very fuzzy and odd version of NPR (who is this Diana Rehm?).

Eventually when you tire of "Brown Eyed Girl" and a staticky "All Things Considered" you will turn the dial to a country music station for a rest and you will get to hear poetic lines like, "Take your tongue out of my mouth I'm kissing you goodbye" and "She's actin' single so I'm drinkin' doubles."

Last summer as we drove around western Michigan my family and I had so much fun listening to these things that we made a list of themes that are featured in almost all country western songs. The best songs manage to incorporate most or all of these themes:

1. She's amazing; I'm a doofus (or variations on this theme such as "I'm lucky she's with me" or "I behaved like an ass and I hope she'll forgive me.")

2. This country is the best country anywhere in the world. So there.

3. I don't have much but I'm happy. So there.

4. I drink a lot of alcohol after work. Usually beer.

5. Poor people have way more fun than rich people. So there.

6. I'm country through and through (even if I live in a Nashville mansion) and that makes me better than you.

7. Blue jeans/women's behinds in blue jeans

8. Pick up trucks

9. Jesus

10. Lil' bitty babies

11. Soldiers (never officers)

I think that covers it.

I know a lot of people like country music and I know a few who pretend they don't but really do but I don't know anyone who pretends to like it if they don't. Do with that what you will.

I honestly don't know if I like it or not but I know it can sure break up a tedious road-trip.

REPORT FROM AMSTERDAM

Today's post is an email I got this morning from Jeff:

We are in Amsterdam. We had quite the travel day yesterday. It took us 4 hours to get here from Brussels by train and I'm pretty sure you can do it in less. I don't know if we screwed up or if it is what it was. Hmmm? The train we were supposed to get on did not arrive as planned. In the meantime, they flashed another train on the sign and a few minutes later a train arrived. Now we have a problem. Is the train that pulled up our train or a different train? We got on and the conductor stamped our tickets so I figured all is well. We arrived in Antwerp (as our train was supposed to) but only after stopping in every small town between Brussels and Antwerp. This is the part that makes me think it could have been the wrong train. When the train stopped in Antwerp everyone got off except me and Grace because our train is going to Amsterdam you see. Funny not a single person on the train except for me and Grace were going to Amsterdam because everyone got off. After twenty minutes of waiting Grace asks the obvious question in only a way that Grace can. Daddy? Why is there no one here and why is the train stopped? I guess this is my hint to go and check it out which I do. It turns out the next train to Amsterdam is two levels below ours and leaves in 25 minutes. So we lost about an hour. This train too stopped many times before we got off.

The walk from the train station to our home the Swiss Hotel is five minutes from the train station but that is only if you know where you are going which we don't. So we start off - the streets are madness - people, bikes, dogs, trams, buses, bums, potheads, AC-DC fans (yes they are in town and the place is abuzz). So Grace is a good sport and just follows 2 feet behind me. Where ever I go, so does she. I think in my head, I just want to get someplace where I won't be trampled and there is a little calm so that I can consult my map. It turns out that is Glenview, not Amsterdam. So I check out the map and we are a little off, so we adjust. We walk through narrow streets with coffee houses and the smell of pot everywhere. Poor Grace I think to myself. The place looks like a shit hole with the lowest of the lows assembled to do nothing more except sit with each other and drink and smoke weed. Almost everyone I see looks like they have not bathed or changed their cloths since they arrived, which could have been some time in 2008. We finally leave that street to go down a quieter and cleaner street and with much fewer people. I breathe a little sigh of relief until I see the girls standing in the windows. Yes, we are in the red light district. But it is clean and it is quiet and no one bothers us. We find our street and finally arrive at the Swiss Hotel in the heart of things but just far enough a way to not feel dangerous.

We got settled and went right out. We had a nice Italian dinner and we ate outside and just had the best time watching the people and the world go by. At least that is my recollection. Grace is a good sport. She does not complain. She tells me when she wants something, but she is satisfied to go to this place or that place or another place if that is where we go. We made

The Ann Frank House our destination and we had a lovely tour. Very moving as you probably remember. We walked back to our home and had ice cream along the way. We got back about 9:30. I took off my shoes and laid on the bed and Grace, God Bless her asks if we are going to go out again or should she put on her pajamas. We decide to make this an early night and I turned out my lights around 10 pm.

THE CHRISTMAS PARTY

On Saturday we held our annual Christmas party for our neighbors and friends in the area. This was our 12th annual event and they have evolved over the years from a casual open house to a big bash with kids invited to the current more intimate but elegant cocktail party (no kids) that we now have for about 40 guests.

We've done this long enough that the party follows a somewhat familiar pattern: 7:00 we stand waiting breathlessly for the guests to arrive, slightly panicked that maybe no one is coming. By 7:15 the first guests arrive and then a steady stream until the house is packed around 9:30. We usually cap out at about 45 people and then they start to drift off, some going home early, others to competing Christmas parties (darn that Khaki Voss who always throws her party the same night as mine! She is one of those incredibly nice people who also happens to do everything just a little better than everyone else and I'm sure she has a lot better food at her party than we do....) but anyhoo the party always finishes off with ten or so lingerers and Jeff and our good buddy Dan get the guitars out and sing and play and things wrap up around 1:00 or 1:30.

This year things went as expected. The only change we made was that I added a new convenient feature out front. I shoveled a spot at the curb and leading up the front walk for the ladies in heels and then, thinking it would be nice to make sure no one blocked the cleared spot I set up two sawhorses in the street with signs that said "Bag Drop" on them. The golfers in the group got it, pulled up and let their "bags" out then went to park. I'm thinking of patenting the idea.

The next morning we always have fun doing post-party debrief, sharing conversations and deciding things like who said stuff they shouldn't have and who wore the most revealing dress. This year (as usual) that would be me and me. The kids chime in and tell us funny things they saw and heard too as they are the official coat-takers and hostess-gift keepers. As Lilly said, "By the end of the night when the grownups came to get their coats they were all standing really close and talking loud."

Over burgers yesterday I even got to hear a story of a past party that I had never heard before. We were talking about party number five in 2003, the last time we invited children. We did that for several years until it got rather "Lord of the Flies"-like and when I went up to bed after that party I found Atticus (who was ten at the time) asleep in the hallway lying with his face in a pile of crushed Goldfish crackers not unlike Al Pacino in Scarface. I just checked my notes—we had 54 adults and 62 kids that year.

We were laughing about all that when Grace said, "Lilly, that's the year you hid in the bathroom and we couldn't find you."

"What?" I asked. This was news to me. We had had babysitters that year to help wrangle the kids so I guess I had missed the parallel kids' party.

"Yeah," she explained, "it was late and the grownups don't usually come upstairs so I ran from my bedroom to the bathroom to go potty in just my underpants but when I opened the door there was a grownup waiting for the bathroom so I slammed the door in his face and locked it."

"We couldn't figure out why that door was locked for so long," Atticus recalled.

"But why did you hide in the cupboard?" Grace asked.

"I was afraid mom might find the key and open the door and grownups would see me in my underwear. So I crawled in the cabinet."

That is not a big vanity—30 inches tops and it would be a tight squeeze even for a small five-year-old.

Ahh, good times.

I like to believe that these big parties with their mishaps and their funny stories that live on for years are as much fun for my kids as they are for us. I can think of no better way to usher in the Christmas week than with a house full of the parents of your friends who make up your world—adults you've known your whole life—all laughing and telling stories and just enjoying each other.

I hope your Christmas and holiday season is also full of love, and laughter, and noise and may you too have your own share of stories of locked bathrooms and crushed Goldfish crackers.

Merry Christmas.

HALLOWEEN: THEN AND NOW

Lately I've been on a "look at how things have changed" jag so at the risk of becoming Andy Rooney-esque I'm going to just keep going today with that theme. Today's topic is Halloween and how it has changed since we were kids. Come along and see if any of this is familiar.

COSTUMES: When we were kids we were either hobos or clowns or if our parents were rich and sprang for one of those lame plastic one-piece costumes we were superman or a princess. If our mother were handy with the sewing machine (and mine was) your repertoire could expand and I was even a pumpkin one year, my mother patiently sewing a many-gored costume she designed herself, but really, that kind of thing was rare. Now all the costumes are awesome. Even the cheapest costume at Target is of far superior quality to anything we had. Babies can be adorable fuzzy ladybugs and older kids can have elaborate horse and rider costumes all at affordable prices. This is all I'm sure due to global trade and I will try not to think about the fact that probably some Chinese waif was paid four or five grains of wheat to sew my kid's bunny suit.

CANDY: Man what was that crap they gave out when we were kids? Good N Plenty? Wax lips? Those god-awful peanut butter chewy things wrapped in orange or black waxed paper? And people were stingy too. None of this fistful of candy. You got one or two per kids. I remember SINGLE servings of Life Savers. I kid you not. Now my kids get handfuls of some of the best chocolate candy they make. Butterfingers, 100,000 bars, 3 Musketeers. The GOOD stuff. I suppose this is just another example of our super-sized mentality that has brought us our super-sized butts but I'll tell you one thing —it makes raiding the kids' candy bag a lot more fun for us.

DECORATIONS: I don't really need to tell you about the explosion of Halloween decorations do I? We all have a neighbor who now puts out more lights, hangs more stuff, and drapes more trees at Halloween than even the craziest of neighbors did at Christmas time when we were kids. Halloween decorations when we were kids? That meant putting out a pumpkin with a candle in it and a paper pumpkin on the doorway that you made at school (unless Ricky Soloway from down the street conned you out of your own paper pumpkin and his mom put it on THEIR door, not saying that ever happened to me or anything but it could and you might even be bitter about it 44 years later).

WEATHER: Now this changes every year of course especially since Al Gore got involved but since my youngest was born we have actually had many, many Halloweens that were fairly warm. Warm enough that you did not need a coat over your costume and that is weird because we live in Chicago. This NEVER happened when I was a kid. If you did not have long underwear AND a winter coat under or over your costume on Halloween you must have lived south of the Mason-Dixon line. And most of those nights it was raining too. Sideways.

SAFETY: In this safety obsessed time when everyone is a stranger and we teach our kids to run screaming from them all it is hard to believe that at least for this one holiday our parents were even more paranoid than we are. That's because back in those days we were taught that there were crazy people who put razor blades in the candy. Our home town police even offered to x-ray the candy before you ate it. To my knowledge they did not once find a pin or a razor blade in the candy. I haven't even heard about this alleged scare in years. What does that mean? Did these crazy razor-blade toting, child-hating people all die off or did they all become strangers trying to lure our kids into cars with puppies? I have no idea.

These are some of the things that have changed over the years but for the most part, around here at least, Halloween looks like it did when I was a kid: Grandmas still open their front door and peer into the dark saying "Oh what a beautiful princess!" and "My what a scary monster!"; preschoolers to preteens still wander the streets past dark, safe for one night to cross the street without looking; and autumn leaves skitter at their feet pushed on by a wind that tells us snow is not far behind. Most of all it is still a magical night when every child gets to dress up and pretend to be anyone or anything he wants while filling up a pillow case with more candy than he could eat in a year.

Happy Halloween!

WHAT WOULD TYRA DO?

When I used to come home from the 7th grade I would grab the box of Ritz Crackers, a tub of port-wine cheese, and head into my bedroom where I would watch re-runs of "Petticoat Junction" on the small black and white TV my parents (surprisingly) allowed me to have in my room. It was in this manner I would forget about the minor mean girl acts and other mini transgressions that are part and parcel of being in junior high.

Lots of curves you bet, even more when you get, to the Junction! Petticoat Junction! Why on earth were those girls allowed to bathe in the water tower? That seems mighty unsanitary.

When Lilly comes home from 7th grade she grabs the pita chips, the hummus and flops down on the couch to watch "The Tyra Show" on the big family-room flat-screen TV.

I'm coming out! I want the world to know, got to let it show! Who are all these horrible people shamelessly talking about the terrible things they do?

It is hard for me to imagine two shows that are more ridiculously different than "Petticoat Junction" and "The Tyra Show."

I don't really get what my daughter likes about this show. Wait she's in the room now, I will ask her.

Okay, here is what she said, "I like the Tyra show because there are a bunch of crazy people on that show and they are entertaining to watch. And because Tyra keeps it real."

I (along with pretty much everyone my age and older) do not like this genre of talk show because I find it horribly depressing to learn that I share the planet let alone the same nationality with said crazy people. People like the woman who weighed 600 pounds and aspires to weigh 1000 pounds. Or the parents who took their gay son to a fringe church to have his "gayness" exorcised (beaten) out of him. Or the woman who brought her husband to the show so she could tell him (in front of a national TV audience) that he no longer excites her sexually (but she just couldn't bring herself to tell him before that point because it might hurt his feelings WTF??).

I know the parenting manual says that when your kid watches a show you do not approve of you are supposed to watch it with her and say things like, "Well what do you think about that?" or "That's interesting do you think he handled that well?"

Instead I shout things like, "Oh for god sakes, what a horrible human!" "Who DOES that?" and "Please tell me this is a bad, bad joke!"

How's that for keeping it real?

But this stuff cracks Lilly up. Perhaps this horrible behavior makes the junior high nonsense look tame. I don't know.

I do know that she takes much of what Tyra says to heart and quotes her which leads to scenes like this:

At dinner: "You took too many potatoes. Tyra says your serving of carbs should be no bigger than your fist."

When I was worrying about going without my wig when my hair first grew out, "You have to just be you and be fierce. That's what Tyra would say. Then she'd look at you and say something nice about you," here Lilly looked me over from top to bottom, obviously searching for something nice to say and finally came up with, "You have nice teeth."

And she has learned a LOT about black women and their hair and hair extensions in general. Which is why our new favorite game to play when we watch TV is "Is she wearing extensions?" It also explains when she told the sweet 8-year-old African-American girl at our church, "I like your hair," and the girl answered, "It ain't mine, it's a weave," she was not a bit surprised.

So I don't like that she watches it but at least she's learning. I don't think I learned anything from "Petticoat Junction" except if I ever get the chance to stay at the Shady Rest I should not drink the water.

THE ARNOLD STORY

(NOTE: Everyone's name in this story has been changed except Arnold, me, and Maria)

Okay, okay now that he's all over the news again I think it is time to reveal my own Arnold story (for the few of you who have not already heard it). Yes, I have met the man—had dinner with him in fact—but I did not have an affair with him.

The year was 1981, the place Madrid. I was there for my junior year abroad. He was there filming Conan the Barbarian (a movie I still have never seen). His cast and crew were living at the Villa Magna, a fancy high-rise near the University and my ex-roommate "Wilma", a fancy girl from Louisville had moved out of our boarding house and into the Villa Magna over the Christmas break. Being blonde and American the Conan Crowd quickly found Wilma and she became friends with a lot of them and had parties with them that we were all invited to or sometimes we just all hung out in the Villa Magna bar.

My friend "Mary" (no that's really her name, she doesn't care if I tell this story) started dating one of the stuntmen, a nice dumb kid from LA whose name I still see in movie credits from time to time. He's the guy in the cowboy hat on the left. The guy on the right is also a stuntman, Tony something. The girls are classmates.

One night that winter, Wilma called me with a last-minute dinner party invitation. She was hosting Arnold and his buddy Franco and Wilma's roommate, "Catherine" (the fabulously wealthy Belgian girl who had been sent to Spain to get over the death of her Grand Prix race-car driver boyfriend who'd been killed in a race....you can't make this stuff up), had to cancel at the last minute. Did I want to come? Heck yes I wanted to come. It was free food and I was always a starving student in those days. It was a low-key night. The guys were exhausted from a tough day of shooting on horseback and I don't remember much about it except that I ate more than either of them which was kind of funny.

The parties were more fun—an eclectic mix of American actors, crew-members from all over, and the students at our Spanish school who were mostly American and European, and our Spanish friends. At one party, I remember, Arnold grabbed Mary's ass as she was introduced to him. This was just his way of being friendly apparently. He also would work out in the apartment gym with my friend Wilma and give her fitness tips that also included a butt-grab—purely technical of course—to demonstrate what she should be working on.

I'm a little sad to say that he never tried to grab my behind. It may be because I was with my Spanish boyfriend when I met him the first time or it may be, as Mary says, he sensed I would deck him if he tried. Of course it can't be because my ass is not grab-worthy—it still is and it surely was in 1981.

Anyhoo, even then there were rumors that he was cheating on Maria (they were not married yet, still dating) with one of the European girls from my school and rumors about his co-star. I've been thinking about all this as the tawdry news unfolds. I remember thinking back then that surely even Maria, a cosmopolitan member of the Kennedy family would not be okay with this. Maybe I should have sent Maria an anonymous letter then. Maybe she could have avoided this.

Who know? She probably has received a lot of anonymous letters over the years and chose to ignore them.

Which is too bad. I feel badly for her, and her children, and the housekeeper, and I feel even worse for the 14-year-old "love child" who surely is the most innocent victim of all in this mess.

But I sure don't feel bad for Arnold. I don't suppose anyone feels bad for him.

Except maybe Tiger.

PART 05: FRIENDS & FAMILY

THE ZOO

"When you write a book about us I want my name to be 'Elizabeth'," my former roommate said at our recent annual reunion. She brings this idea up every year, but I'm not sure what the book might be about. I mean, how much does everyone want to hear about how great my college roommates are and how lucky I am that the eight of us are all still in touch?

Well, maybe you'd like to hear a little, so I'll blog about them.

First, I have to tell you that we all met (for the most part) our freshman year at the University of Michigan. We all had come to Ann Arbor knowing next to no one. We lived on the fifth floor of Williams house in West Quad and soon found out everyone referred to our hall as "the zoo" as it had until recently been where the football players lived and since they acted like animals — well they got the nickname. People would say, "Oh you live up in the zoo" and after awhile we just started calling ourselves that. We even had sweatshirts made to look like a sorority sweatshirts with the Zeta Omicron Omicron letters on the front. We were well-known for having parties with way too many men and too few women. It was a formula that worked for us.

We have been getting together nearly every year for the past 25 years. We are all in long-term marriages (mine is the longest I think at 27) and we all have kids. Between us we have 20 children (four of whom are named Nicholas) and 3 step-children and too many college degrees to keep track of including one MD, two RNs, three MBAs, one MA in landscape architecture, and a degree in international finance (there are more as some of us have multiples but you get the idea).

When we get together we do pretty much the same thing every year, as follows:

1. Tell the same stories: most of the stories are about boys in our past. Who went out with whom, who moved where to follow a boy, who was found in a closet with whom at which party etc. Sometimes, since we mix stuff up over time we need to untangle entire sagas. Three of the guys we knew in college are now husbands. There is some overlap.

2. Laugh until we pee: usually this happens when one of us says something ridiculously funny (unintentionally). This year that award went to the following exchange: "Has anyone gone through the change yet?" "I sure went through the change on that toll-road."

3. Cry: We don't always cry but we do when someone has had a tough year or a tough loss such as a parent, a sibling, or a pet. This year someone had a sad story about a life-threatening illness she's been battling. So we cried.

4. Discuss who we would like to have sex with if we were gay: Ever since one of us came out of the closet years ago, we feel, for some reason, compelled to have this discussion. This year, I have to say almost everyone agreed on Kalinda from "The Good Wife" and Gwyneth Paltrow.

So there you have it. A brief discussion, if not a full novel on my awesome college friends. Some day I may write that novel. I could start with the story of a beautiful blonde with dazzling blue eyes from Traverse City named "Elizabeth" who grew up to marry the dashing international financier "John" with even bluer eyes and they had three children, one of whom got mixed up in a banana caper.... well you'll have to wait for the novel to see how that goes.

FRIENDS' PARENTS AND PARENTS' FRIENDS

Mr. E., the father of Lilly's BFF Danielle, is like a character in a movie to Lilly. He even has a tagline—whenever she calls he sings into the phone, "Lilly Ludwig—Lilly Ludwig—Lilly Lilly Lilly" before he goes to get Danielle. And ever since big sister Grace gave a speech at the eighth grade graduation last spring he brings it up whenever Lilly visits. "That sister of yours—she's going places. She can give a great speech. Wonderful skill. Alexander," here he pauses to look at his own offspring, same age as Grace, "You should be able to give a speech like Grace. That girl is going places." And as if that were not enough fodder to entertain Lilly for hours (she is a great mimic) Lilly went sailing with the family this fall and every time Mr. E. found a piece of litter in Lake Michigan he would head the boat toward it, fish it out of the water and hold it aloft shouting to the world at large, "This is nature's playground people! Is this how you treat it?"

When Lilly tells me all of this I am reminded of that wonderful, mythical creature of my own childhood—my friends' parents. I remember them all so clearly and with great fondness and amusement.

There was Mr. K. who was the nutty community college professor who seemed to have disdain for anyone less intelligent than him (or is it he? this would make him crazy) and his equally brilliant wife Mrs. K. who loved to do jigsaw puzzles then shellac them and hang them on the walls. The K. family thrived on order and predictability and actually had the same meal schedule every week. Monday was chicken, Tuesday meatloaf and so on. I loved that I could always get my favorite meal—a BLT on any given Friday of my entire junior and high school career.

I grew up next door to my best friend Jenny S. Her dad was a huge man with a perverse sense of humor. He told his kids outrageous lies like "Eat the burned toast, it will clear up your acne." Once, returning from an excursion to see the fireworks they shoot over the Detroit river (we had been on the Canadian side) we got stuck for hours on the Ambassador Bridge. Both Jack (his son) and I desperately had to use the bathroom. Instead of trying to find a place for us to relieve ourselves or reassuring us he kept saying, "Think of running water, kids!" "Try to focus on sprinkling fountains!"

Equally intriguing were those people we saw less frequently but were no less mythic: the friends of our parents. Mr. and Mrs. W. who did not have children but had a poodle named FiFi who had *her own bedroom with a pink princess phone*! They were impossibly glamorous: they only drove Cadillacs and smoked cigarettes and Mrs. W. always left a smear of lipstick on her cocktail glass. And Mr. D. the three (plus) martini lunch man who occasionally called late at night, waking my parents to invite my father to join him at the bar. He was one of the original Mad Men.

In college I met a whole new cast of friends' parents, widening my circle. I was especially fond of Mr. and Mrs. D. Both were fabulously brilliant people of wit and words. A sort of Nick and Nora of Southfield Michigan. He was an editor for the AP and she was a Smith grad, something I'd barely heard of until I met her. They both smoked and could do the New York Times Sunday crossword puzzle in ink and drank whiskey sours. I adored them both as they were the kind of couple who made you feel like they were just sitting by the fire waiting for you to drop in on them at any time.

As I go over all the parents of my friends in my mind I realize many of them stood just in front of a shadow I only glimpsed from time to time. As a guest in a friends' house, a child sees just a bit more than an adult would and I was aware even as a kid that sometimes something else was going on in a home. As an adult I now know there were in many households struggles with alcohol, marital problems, eating disorders, and abuse. But as a kid I never thought to ask about it or judge it—it was just there.

It is hard for me to believe that we are now the friends' parents and the parents' friends of many. What do they see when we are around or are being talked about? I know Jeff has gone a long way toward being an eccentric memory for our children's friends: between the fact that he never puts his guitar down and that he sings with great gusto as he plays and that he insists on greeting every child who enters our home with a conversation stopping, "So, tell me a story!" (he thinks this is a conversation starter) he is well on his way to being frozen as a childhood memory for some.

I do not really know how I am viewed by my children's friends. I just hope I am memorable enough to some day be immortalized as one of these great and mythical creatures—a friend's parent.

IT'S ALL RELATIVE

A while back I was chatting with my parents in my kitchen about a family event. We were trying to remember when it took place. Finally, I said, "I think it wasn't that long ago. Maybe two years." My parents nodded. Lilly, who had been playing with her plastic horses and eavesdropping looked up in horror.

"Not too long ago? Two years!?"

"Well, that does seem like a long time when you're only 11 but when you're older it seems like a short time, like maybe a few months feels to you," I tried to explain. "Isn't that how it is for you, Grandpa?"

"No," my father replied, "Two years is more like a long afternoon for me."

Indeed. If we are to believe Einstein (and why wouldn't we?) time is relative. And so Lilly's two years represent nearly 20% of her life and a mere 2.5% of my father's life.

As anyone over the age of 12 knows, time accelerates as you get older until one day you are 49 and you say things like, "I saw him not so long ago at the 20th class reunion," and realize that was more than a decade ago.

My father called me on my birthday this year and said, "Well, this is a big one for you!"

"No," I reminded him, "I'm 49, next year will be the big one."

"Right, I know. But that's just around the corner."

EEK.

These time/age games can be fun and alarming to play. Let's look at the year 1994. You remember that year pretty clearly, right? It was 15 years ago but that's not so long—True Lies was at the movies and Bill Clinton was our president and Sheryl Crow sang, "All I wanna do". Hardly ancient history, right? Compare that to what was going on 15 years before the year you were born. Go ahead, I'll wait while you do the math. Wait, how can that be? I was born in 1960 so fifteen years before that—World War II was ending. WHAT? Wasn't World War II like in the 1800's or something?

Nothing makes you feel that time flying past you faster than having kids. In a blink they are babies, toddlers, preschoolers. Now it's even faster; junior high, homecoming, learning to drive. I feel like the ride that is parenthood has sped up from a jaunty merry-go-round to a zero-gravity space ship in which your cheeks fly back as the rocket takes off.

If only I had some meaningful interpretation of today's ramblings but I really have not much more to offer than the obvious. Life is short. It gets shorter every second.

So enjoy this summer day and enjoy Joni Mitchell as she sings the best song ever about time passing.

PURE MICHIGAN

A while back I got an email from my high-school Spanish teacher entitled "You might be from Michigan if...." I forwarded it to Beth who I met here in Chicago but is also from Michigan. She replied "If you still keep in touch with your high-school Spanish teacher, you might be from Michigan."

Well I am from Michigan and I do know how to play and SPELL euchre and I do point at my hand when you ask me where I am from. I love those Pure Michigan take-off ads. If you haven't seen them check this one out about University of Michigan football fans. Warning, if you actually went to UofM you may snort food out of your nose laughing when you see this so make sure you are not eating.

My kids like to point out things that they consider to be Pure Michigan when we travel there. Like the enormous woman at Culvers who brought her cheese curds in to the bathroom with her and kept eating while waiting in the bathroom line. Lilly spotted this delightful creature and told me about it in the car saying, "I was afraid she might eat me, so I got out of there. Pure Michigan."

Or last summer when we went to the fancy horse show in Traverse City. When we went to get a pop (not soda, we were in Michigan) we saw a dad on an ATV with his kid on the back. The kid who was about seven had a rattail (I think that is what that fashion statement hair-style is called) and the dad was holding a beer while he drove around the grounds. "Pure Michigan" Lilly whispered.

Last weekend Jeff and I had dinner with my old high school boyfriend Greg who lives with his wife Sue in the Chicago suburbs like everyone else who moved away after college. The fact that we had dinner with them might be Pure Michigan—I'm not sure. Anyhoo, he and I got to reminiscing about our old high school which has been demolished and replaced with a Taj-Mah-High-School as my sister calls it.

"You know, they built that new school on our old cornfield," I said to Greg referring to a favorite make-out spot.

"Hey, is that the same cornfield you took me to?" his wife of 25+ years asked.

Making out in cornfields. Pure Michigan.

Although I bet they have those in Iowa and Wisconsin too.

Pure Midwest.

TEXTING 1-2-3

Today's post comes to you courtesy of Lilly, my 13-year-old. Basically, I will just post a text she sent me and you will laugh and I will not have to write much at all.

I just need to set it up.

So last week she wanted to go on a sleep-over. She's not a big sleep-over kid and it was at the home of some friends I don't know well in a neighborhood I am not familiar with. So naturally I had a lot of questions, most of which are pretty useless because in the end you let them go but it's what you do when you're a mom and want to at least pretend you have some control over a situation.

Me: Are you sure you want to sleep over? You aren't big on that.

Lilly: Yeah, I really want to. By the way, they have an indoor pool and want to know if it's okay with you to swim.

Me: Umm, I guess. But you aren't a strong swimmer. Who will supervise?

Lilly: *(rolling her eyes)* We're 13 there will be no supervisors. Do you send a supervisor with me to the community pool?

Me: Uhh, I guess not. Can you at least have a swim buddy? You know, just tell a friend you aren't a great swimmer and it's her job to keep an eye on you.

Lilly: Yeah. Yeah I'll do that *(making a face that clearly says she would not do that if I put a gun to her head)*. Geez, when did you become Tiger Mom?

Me: It's just that, you know, that's the neighborhood where the candy heiress, Helen Brach disappeared.

Lilly: When?

Me: 1977.

Lilly: Yeah. Bad neighborhood.

In the end we sent her off to the sleep over in the mansion. A real mansion by the way, not a McMansion. Later that night I texted her and asked if she was okay. Here is her response:

Text: Well, we had to fend off many murderous multi-billionaires and the waters in the pool were rough. But no worries. Not dead yet. I informed Mrs. Levi that she must supervise me at all times (even when we are sleeping) and told the other kids not to rough house in the shallow end where I have been all night. I also reminded them we can only watch something rated G...maybe PG if we are feeling up to something on the raunchy side. Oh yes, and I also reminded them that Jesus Christ is my savior, since they are Jewish and all. So there are no issues.

Good night, Mommy.

Good night, Lilly.

MICHAEL JOHNSON

About sixty years ago, when Jeff and I were first married, we went to dinner at the home of some friends of my parents'—Art and Sondra. They were older than us. Really old. They were, let's see carry the one divide by...they were about my age now. But they were always fun (still are) and made us nice food and drinks so we loved to see them.

As we got a tour of their grown-up home full of teenaged children we came to one of the daughter's rooms. She had a poster on the wall and Art said, "Oh yeah, that's that singer Michael Johnson." This SLAYED us! It was the early 80s and the poster was of course of Michael Jackson. We made fun of Art and then later laughed about it more. In fact, we laughed about it for *years* assuming that old people just don't know who pop singers are.

But lately, I am not laughing so hard. Because it turns out, this happens to all of us. After filling our brains with useless things like the names of the Brady Bunch (Greg, Peter, Bobby, Marcia, Jan, and Cindy) you find the names of more recent celebs tend to not fit in there. You will not be able to fit Kylie Minogue and Nikki Minaj and actually know the difference. And forget trying to put Kardashian names in there, you have stuffed that space with Shaun and David Cassidy.

On Saturday I came in the house and said to Lilly, "I was just listening to the funniest interview on NPR with Justin *Timberfield*." As soon as it was out of my mouth I knew it was wrong. I sort of looked at the malaprop as it slipped to the floor. Then I looked her in the eyes, praying she hadn't caught it but I could tell by the snarky smile forming at her lips I would have no luck sneaking it by. I came clean. "Did I just say Justin Timberfield," heh heh, I laughed nervously." Aren't I funny?"

A few weeks ago I was on the phone with my mom. She was telling me about my sister's trip to New York City, "Yes, she went to see the spot where George Hamilton was shot." Umm, what? "You know, the Beatle." I whooped at this, "Mom," I said, rolling my eyes as Lilly does to me, "George Hamilton is the tan actor your age, I think you mean George Harrison." Of course it was two hours later when I told the story to Jeff that he had to remind me I meant John Lennon. Oh. Right. Shit. When I told my friend Beth this story she pointed out helpfully that at least I didn't think she meant Alexander Hamilton who was shot by some vice president...was that Dick Cheney?

Then Beth suggested we could have a game show for older people in which you say things like "What is the name of the actor who starred in 'Love at First Bite'" and then one of you would say, "Wasn't that girl from 'McMillan and Wife' in that movie?" and "I think he was on 'Dancing with the Stars'" and another would say "And that movie about spring break where boys are, what's the name of that movie?" and the other old person would say "Where the Boys Are" and the first would say, "Yes, I know that's what it's about but what's the name of the movie?" and so on and so on until the game show host's ears would bleed and no one ever would come up with George

Hamilton unless my mother was there and she could say "Wasn't he shot in front of The Dakota?" And the funniest part of all is that ALL of the older people will TOTALLY follow this conversation like a lot of you just did.

So there you go. You can make fun of older people but then one day you're older too and you'll have these silly half conversations and it will be oddly comforting.

CRUSHES

I am a fan of a good-old-fashioned full-on crush. I think my first crushes were in the fifth grade (Peter Duel from "Alias Smith and Jones" and Larry Brown from school) and by high school I had two or three at a time. I would walk clear around the building if I had to just to get a glimpse of my crush between classes. Sometimes they were boys I knew and actually spoke to. Sometimes they were upper classmen who did not know I existed. I had so many crushes that at the 30th reunion last summer I would have to say the only man in the room I had not had a crush on at some point was the bartender (though he was a handsome devil).

Then there were the "girl-crushes". I'm so glad there's a term for this now because when I was young, back in the good old homo-phobic days, this was not something you voiced. Usually I had girl crushes on girls who were sort of famous in my hometown, say the homecoming queen or the girl who always had the lead in the play. Girl crushes are non-sexual—you just can't stop looking at and admiring these people. Like Princess Di. That crush lasted a good decade.

I mentioned this once to my friend K. who knew exactly what I was talking about. She had had an enormous crush on a girl from her hometown who was a high school actress and performer. At the time, K. was still in junior high and after seeing this girl once, she was smitten. She would beg her parents to take her to any performance the girl was in and record them with her little portable tape-recorder. The fervor of a junior high crush is a powerful thing.

All these years later I have to say I still get crushes. I felt one coming on as I watched the high school musical this spring starring JS (I won't print his name here on the off-chance that he should Google himself (older readers that's not what you think it is) and find out an old lady has a crush on him because that would make him physically ill) (You know this way of speaking with parentheses inside parentheses is exactly how my Dutch friend Laurent speaks; you can almost see the parentheses when he talks).

Anyhoo, about my new crush on JS, star of high school productions...I have to clarify, I do not have a crush on him in a MaryKay Latourneau way, it's in a "I remember what it was like to be 17 and have a crush like this" way. I asked Grace the other day which was more disturbing, my crush on Beyonce or the one I have on JS. She just giggled because like everyone else in town, she has a crush on JS too.

Of course I also have a crush on Barack Obama. Well, who doesn't? And Michelle. In fact this crush has manifested itself into a game I play with Lilly (who has a girl crush on Malia) in which we pretend the Obamas are our friends. "Mr. and Mrs. Obama are coming over to play euchre on Saturday? Do you and Malia want to have a sleep over?" I'll say. "Oh is he back from Egypt already?" Lilly will answer. Then she'll say, "Yeah I'd like to have a sleepover. I'll ask Malia at lunch tomorrow!" (in our little fantasy they go to school together too—hey why not, it's our fantasy). Is that wrong? Do you think some poor Secret Service agent has to read all the blog posts out there to find out which of us has a crush and which of is is actually a threat? God I hope not.

Crushes are healthy. You should not try to deny them even if you are happily married. Of course, they are like a little spark which is a good thing as long as you do not fan it into a flame. You should not hold dry tinder next to them and flirt shamelessly with them. Nor, (if I may carry this metaphor too far) should you throw gasoline on them and share your crush with the crushee. No. That is a bad idea. But if you try to repress a crush by denying to yourself that it exists it will eventually come out in an unhealthy way and the top of your head may explode or if you're a Baptist minister you will run away with the church organist (geez it was just a crush, you weren't supposed to do that!).

So today, go ahead and admit to yourself you have a little crush on the girl who makes your latte or the guy who rides the train or Zac Efron or Taylor Swift (two more of my crushes by the way). It's healthy.
Just don't tell them about it. That's creepy.

DON'T ASK DON'T TELL

I'm on my way to Baltimore to celebrate the marriage of my dear friends Anna and Julie. I post this in their honor. Long after many a hereto marriage has disintegrated, they will still be together, exemplifying what a wonderful, strong, God-filled marriage looks like. Bless you both.

Apparently, this topic of gay marriage is rather controversial. I am told. Often I hear otherwise sane people say "Well I don't have a problem with them being gay, I just don't want to know about it. I don't want to know about anyone's sex life! It makes me uncomfortable."

And we wouldn't want that would we? We don't want anyone to be uncomfortable. So for all of you with delicate sensibilities, I suggest a Don't Ask Don't Tell policy that applies to us all equally.

From this day forward, none of us, gay, straight, lesbian, whatever, will discuss our "sex life" as you put it.

Beginning immediately, you must:

1. Stop talking about your spouse in any way that might let us know you are more than friends. please don't mention he snores or that he sometimes walks around in his underwear. If we know that then our minds might wander to the fact that you are intimate and that makes us uncomfortable.

For some of you, it even grosses us out, frankly. Refer to your spouse as "your friend" so you don't offend anyone.

2. No longer attend weddings or celebrate anniversaries. These events acknowledge that you are a couple and probably share a bed and we all know what that means and we don't want to think about it.

3. Take down the pictures of your spouse you have at work. No one wants to know that he is more than just a friend to you. Also get rid of the pictures of your kids. When we see you have kids we know you had sex and that is something we are very uncomfortable thinking about.

4. Never hug, hold hands or for god's sake kiss your spouse in public. This includes in front of family and friends because it makes a lot of people uncomfortable. Really, we don't need to know about your sex life!

5. If your husband leaves you tomorrow, you are not entitled to anything because the law no longer recognizes that you are a couple. That's because if they recognize you are a couple, the law would also recognize you have sex, and we don't want to know about anyone's sex life.

6. If you go to the hospital your spouse will not be able to find out how you are doing. He can only find that out through blood relatives like your parents and siblings. I think you know why.

If this all seems ridiculous, then ask yourself, why do you expect this from our gay and lesbian brothers and sisters?

Peace and blessings to all married couples today. What God has joined, let no one put asunder.

JUST HOLD A TOWEL OVER THE WINDOW

I should be out grocery shopping and getting ready for the Thanksgiving crowd I am hosting this Thursday but instead I am waiting for an auto mechanic who makes house calls to come help me. My ten-year-old minivan refuses to start today. Well, technically, she can start—the problem is the key no longer turns in the ignition. Alas it is not a simple fix—the spare keys don't work either which means the key isn't worn out but the ignition is and banging on it with a hammer is not working.

My kids keep telling me we need a new minivan. I say, "You're a bunch of wimps." They have no idea what it's like to drive a real beater around. Right now the only thing wrong with my car (except for the aforementioned issue) is that the passenger window rolls down but doesn't always roll up. Which is why I say, "Quite whining and hold a towel over the window" when it rains. Usually it will roll back up but only after you drive around a bit pretending you don't care that the elements are coming in on you. The back wiper doesn't work either but so what? How many cars actually have back wipers anyway? The trunk latch broke a few months ago but I did replace that. You really can't have a mini van without the use of a trunk.

Other than that for a ten-year-old car with 100,000 mile on it, it goes great. It is NOT anywhere near the clunker/replace it now stage—and believe me I know.

My first car ever was a used Ford Fiesta my parents bought me when I graduated from college. Now that car sucked. It had fuses that blew if I made a left hand turn with the radio on (I knew how to change them without stopping, they were in the dashboard) and the gas gauge never worked so of course I was frequently running out of gas because I had miscalculated how far a tank of gas would go. It broke down constantly and was so poorly designed you had to pull the engine to do even minor repairs. In case you have never heard the words "pull the engine" let me translate. It means "will cost way more money than you have and take days to repair."

It is one of life's sad truths that only people without much money drive shitty cars that need a lot of money to repair regularly which is why I finally got rid of the car when they told me they had to "pull the engine" to change the oil. I am only exaggerating slightly on that.

My second car was a used Toyota Corolla. It was awesome! It NEVER broke down and the only money I put into it was for brakes. I would still have that car if I hadn't had kids. I can only imagine their complaining if I did still have it. It had vinyl seats, no air-conditioning, crank windows and NO radio which believe me you do not miss as much as you think you'd might. It was a stick shift (which I happen to drive with amazing skill if I do say so myself) and I loved tooling around in that.

Between the Corolla and the mini-van I bought my parents used Buick LeSabre. I know, it looked funny to see me get out of a Grandpa car with my two toddlers in their car seats but that was a nice car too. Very comfy and plush. The only thing was that after driving the Corolla with the manual, that thing was like driving a La-Z-Boy with wheels. Comfortable but boring.

I happily traded that up for my only new car—the now old mini-van and I've been very satisfied with that since. It does the trick when you have kids and it's a Toyota so it doesn't break down.

I had to borrow Coffee Friend 2's car this morning to go to a school appointment and she told me, "Why don't you quit being a cheap hippie and get rid of that piece of shit car before you break down on Lake Avenue like trash." Really. She says stuff like that to me all the time which is why she's one of my favorite people in the world.

But the fact is that even though I can afford a new car (or at least a new used car) I just don't know what I'd get. I still need a minivan and really, who gets rid of a car just because it rains inside occasionally or you can't turn it on when you need it.

Not me.

Happy Thanksgiving everyone! I am thankful I have a minivan and I can afford to repair it when it breaks down!

I WANNA HOLD YOUR HAND

"I saw you and Jeff going for a walk the other day, holding hands so cute," Coffee Friend 2 says, almost accusingly.

I am confused so I say, "Don't you and your husband hold hands when you go for a walk?"

"It would NEVER occur to me," she says emphatically.

Hmm. This is very funny to me as she is Italian and she and her hubby are big huggers and her husband even kisses the men he greets on the cheek but they don't hold hands?

So in my late 40's I noticed for the first time that not all couples hold hands. Weird. In my family everyone holds hands. Married couples, parents and children, young siblings.

Lately my hand has been getting held less though. First Grace and now Lilly have announced they are too old to hold my hand in public. Atticus — well I don't think I've held his hand since he was 3.

I understand of course. You can't very well go to your sixth grade conference holding your mommy's hand but still, after reaching for a child's hand for sixteen years and always finding one it's a bit unnerving to reach out and grab only air.

Today in the van on the way to school I asked Lilly for a stealth hand-hold. She complied but only after making sure the angle of our arms would not give us away to any casual observer driving by.

Is this what parenthood is ultimately about? Forming incredibly tight attachments and bonds the first ten years and then learning to untangle them and let go for the next 50?

When I dropped her at the school door she turned her face in my direction. I no longer expect a kiss goodbye but at least she looked at me and smiled and thanked me for the ride. This is more than I get from my two high-schoolers. I notice they are nearly out the door before the van comes to rest, eager to start their day in their own world, shouting goodbye over their shoulders.

Which is all just how it should be and though we grieve all endings I am left in a lovely place, where this all began. Holding Jeff's hand.

SMILE FOR THE CAMERA

"I don't see you on the schedule," I said frowning at my list of names. It was church-directory picture-taking week last month and I had offered to help register families as they came in all shiny and well-combed and neat. I was talking to a long-time parishioner so I was confused as to why her family's label was missing.

She waved my concern away, "Oh that's because we were here earlier in the week and it didn't go well. The boys had a meltdown, my husband complained, and I ended up in tears so we had to just leave."

Ah, the family portrait. Good times.

If you want to see a middle-aged mom roll her eyes, just ask her about the last time she tried to get her family together for a formal photo.

As every mother knows, it is exceedingly challenging to wrangle all the members of your family for this seemingly simple task. Whether you are dealing with colicky babies, cranky toddlers, or busy, busy, teenagers, it is a Sisyphean chore to get them all in one spot at one time looking well-dressed and well-groomed and not crying.

I don't know why we even try.

Yes I do. It's because one of our jobs is to curate an archive of the family history and a formal family portrait every few years is a big part of the exhibit.

When the kids were little I went for the old dress-em-all-alike look which involved weeks of scouring Target for similar outfits. What a colossal waste of time.

Even after making sure I had something that fit each and every one of us (sometime this process took so long someone outgrew something) and finding a time when no one was napping and dad was home, I would still meet with resistance from the crowd.

Really? Is it so much to ask that you people put the outfit on that I laid out for you on your bed and go smile at the camera for half an hour?

"Do I have to go get my picture taken! I don't wanna. I don't wanna wear jeans and a black t-shirt like everyone else," the whining would begin. The kids were worse.

So in recent years I've adopted the "I don't care what you're wearing, just comb your hair and let's go" policy. Which you think would take care of all the problems and resistance but no, just as you get to this point, the kids will be teenagers and have all kinds of school and after-school activities to conflict with a scheduled photo time.

This year I rescheduled our time slot three times to accommodate the work-choir-horseback riding commitments of my brood. I wasn't quite ready to adopt my friend Laura's policy—"I just scheduled a time and figured it was like dinner on any given night—whoever shows up is in."

This time around I was introduced to a new wrinkle in the whole process—with kids headed off to college it is even less likely you will be able to pull off a complete family portrait.

Mom friends told me their college children had expressed disbelief and even outrage that they would not be in the church directory. One mom said she had a different shot of the family taken and submitted it to accommodate their college kid. Another one submitted their college student's picture separately.

So as we four who were once five stood fake smiling I said a little sadly, "This is weird without Atticus."

But Grace was more pragmatic, "This is who we are now. Let's just take the picture."

Which I think is the perfect sentiment of any formal family picture and a gentle reminder of the ever-changing nature of family.

This is who we are now.

PART 06: RANDOM

MY DOG TELLS YOU ABOUT THE SKUNK

NOTE: *Today's post is written by my dog Molly*

Oh my gosh it was the most awesome best super coolest thing that ever ever happened to me. I call it "the night I finally caught an animal in my mouth."

I'm not saying I've NEVER caught anything but well, okay, I've never caught anything.

Every day I try. I really do. There's this squirrel that lives out on the woodpile and if I can get Mom to open the door at just the right time I can scare the crap out of that thing, chasing it through the yard while it chatters and yells at me up top of the fence. But I can't catch it. It's too fast.

Mom always says, "Go get her! Go get your squirrel friend," she thinks that's really funny. But I never catch her.

Once I caught a delicious dead thing from behind the shed. I took it to Mom but she did not like it and screamed and made me drop it. She called it a mold or something. Dad just went out and took it away so I did not even have a chance to grab it by the neck and rip it to shreds the way I practice on all my stuffed toys.

But that night, last August, I caught a big black thing with two white lines on its back and it was ALIVE!

I almost didn't get the chance. Mom quit letting me out after dark unless I'm on a leash for some reason late this summer. I heard her tell my human brother and sisters I couldn't go out after dark. I don't know why. I'm not scared. And I see great in the dark. But she said it was a bad idea.

So I just waited until she was having one of those drinks Dad makes her in a triangle-shaped glass. After she has one of those she kind of forgets things. It worked. I waited until Dad did something real funny and she laughed and then I asked real politely to go outside. She got up and opened up the door to let me out like she did not even remember she just told the kids not to do that an hour before.

I took off like a shot to the back of the yard where all the animals hide at night. Mom started screaming then but nothing could have stopped me. She was screaming "Molly, NOOOOOOO. SKUUUUUNKKKKK!!"

I could see it out by the back bushes. Kind of fluffy and pretty. All tempting with it's big black and white tail. I caught it easy. It was not fast at all and it couldn't jump up on the fence like that squirrel does.

I had it in my mouth so of course I took it right to Mom on the patio. My plan was to shake the hell out of it, break it's neck, then tear it's throat open!

I don't know what I would do after that, but I practice doing that ALL the time on stuffed animals and I knew it was just what I was supposed to do with that thing. It was all wiggly in my mouth and I liked that even more. Those dumb stuffed animals don't move when I grab them at all!

But then something really weird happened. Some kind of yellow, stinky wet stuff got all over me! I have NO idea where it came from, but it was so smelly and so yucky I had to drop the stripey animal I finally caught. That stuff (it was yellow and got in my eyes and on my neck!) must have come down out of the tree I was standing next to. Or maybe Mom threw it at me or something to get me to drop the stripey live animal. I don't know but it was NASTY!

Mom was screaming. Dad was screaming. Man were they excited and proud of me to finally have caught a real live animal IN MY MOUTH!

But because of that really weird spray thing that came from nowhere I had to go in right then and take a bath. A really long bath. Then mom gave me another bath. Then Lilly gave me a bath. Then they made me sleep in the bathroom all night. I didn't want to sleep in the bathroom but I could tell everyone was kind of mad about the smelly yellow stuff so I didn't complain.

The next day I went looking for my stripey friend but I have not seen it since then. Maybe it moved to someone else's backyard. I wish it would come back. I would LOVE to catch it again. IN MY MOUTH.

I had to have about eleventy dozen more baths and you know what I still smell a little like that weird tree smell or whatever. And it's been weeks now. I don't mind the smell anymore because it reminds me of the best night of my life ever. The night I finally caught something LIVE IN MY MOUTH!

And I can tell you too, if I EVER get the chance to catch another stripey thing in my mouth LIVE, I will totally try it again.

Because that was the best thing that ever happened to me.

BEAUTY AND SHORT HAIR

The prettiest girl in my class back in the olden days of the late 70s was Amy Fitzpatrick. She had this adorable, short bob, with shiny black hair and a natural white streak just to the side of her face. In fact, when I think about it, most of the pretty girls in my class of 78 at Northville High School had short hair.

I was thinking about this because when I attend events at my kids' high school or when I watch TV shows with teenage girls and young women I almost NEVER see girls with short hair. And that got me thinking about the fact that not only did we have short hair but we didn't really wear much makeup. And we wore overalls, a style I am very thankful to say has not really made much of a come back over the years (although I did think I was adorable in my white painter-pant overalls and YES Andie Conder you WERE adorable in yours too).

Here's a nice example of a cute, short-haired girl who is my age, back in the day. She's Lady Grantham now in case you wondered:

At dinner the other night I mentioned this observation to my two long-haired, well-made up teenage daughters and Lilly said, "So, like what makeup did you wear the day you got married?"

"Mascara," I replied.

"And what else?"

"Just mascara. But I think I used a curling iron," I said, feebly.

This was kind of shocking and a bit hilarious to them both.

"Not even some eyeliner?" Grace asked.

"Nope. Even the girls who did wear 'a lot' of makeup did not wear eyeliner. Just a lot of blue eyeshadow and lots of lip gloss."

Now-a-days even the youngest teen girls (not all, but many) have a working knowledge of eyeliner.

And then there is all that hair. Long hair was still popular too in my day but not tons and tons and tons of it. Extensions had not been invented so except for the odd slightly freaky girl who was going for the Crystal Gayle look (below) hair didn't go much past the shoulders.

I noticed that cute little Hayden Panettiere on "Nashville" plays a character who routinely wears her hair in three different lengths—her own (I assume), her longer going-out-in-public extensions, and then her even longer performing-on stage-extensions.

When she wears them at her longest, especially given she is petite, she kind of looks like Cousin It. Actually, so does her co-star, Connie Britton. That is a lot of hair between the two of them. You could coif half of St. Jude's with those extensions.

I believe you are always attracted to the look that was in when you came of age. That is probably why I still find boys with feathered hair kind of foxy. Like Shaun Cassidy. Just kidding, NO ONE has that hair anymore. By the way, do yourself a favor and DO NOT GOOGLE what he looks like now.

And why I think the most beautiful women in Hollywood are Halle Berry, Anne Hathaway (with short hair), and Heath Ledgers girlfriend.

This short hair, no makeup thing was really only a "thing" for a short time and if you look back at the past century really was the only time it was in for women to dress like ten-year-old boys.

Come to think of it, this also explains why I had no idea what a Lesbian looked like until well into my 30s because we all looked like Lesbians.

I'm not saying one way is better or not. I enjoyed the low-pressure almost non-existent grooming days (don't get me started on teeth whitening and body-hair removal) when I was a teen and in college but on the other hand, I kind of wish I had worn a *little* makeup and not sported a mullet in my wedding photos.

How about you? What look is still adorable to you because it was "in" even though it is most decidedly "out"? And what looks kind of ridiculous but is very "in" right now?

BE KIND ON THURSDAY

On Thursday, you may find yourself seated at a table next to someone who does not eat meat. Yes, that means, this person, may indeed say "no thank you" as the turkey is passed around the table.

Rest assured, this person, will (in all likelihood) NOT try to keep you from eating your own turkey. In fact, she will probably not say a thing as she hands you the platter of meat despite the fact that she could tell you some really horrifying things about how the turkey ended up on your table.

So extend her the same courtesy and don't try to discuss her food choice.

I live with two vegetarians now. Both have come to this point after much thoughtful consideration and yes they have indeed considered their protein intake and even what the Bible says about eating meat although I don't know of any other time the Bible is consulted about what to eat for most Protestants.

Anyway, I just ask that you try to be courteous on Thursday and not comment on the whole thing. For some reason, this seems to be a fun pastime for some uncles and grandpas and even dads.

So maybe it's time for a quick review on how to eat around a vegetarian....yep, this last part is a reprint as I am under the weather and have been for some time. But here goes.Let me explain her decision quite simply: she does not eat animals for the same reason you do not cook your dog for dinner.

She kind of has the high ground on this one—there is no moral reason at all that we eat cows and pigs but not cats and dogs. It's just our culture. And I probably don't have to remind you that cows and pigs aren't exactly treated as well as our cats and dogs prior to their slaughter. So you can see her point, even if you don't want to stop eating meat yourself.

Now I know you don't want to be one of those people who responds in a goofy manner so I will give you a few tips you might use Thursday:

1. **Please don't ask why she is a vegetarian**: I know, I used to do this all the time too thinking I was making clever conversation—but the fact is most vegetarians have chosen not to eat meat for ethical reasons not health reasons so there's your answer. Additionally, it is just more polite not to require an explanation for the same reason you are not required to explain why you put so much butter on your potatoes. It is tiresome.

2. **Don't worry about the protein**: People, adults especially, like to tell vegetarians they won't get enough protein if they don't eat meat. This is a big fat myth. The American diet is loaded with protein. If you eat an egg for

breakfast, a piece of cheese for lunch, and some beans for dinner you have just had more protein than most of the world has in a week.

3. **Don't worry about what to feed a vegetarian**: Hostesses often stress over this, "But what does she eat!" Umm, let's review...EVERYTHING but meat. You do not need to make a tofu turkey or anything, she'll eat the veggies and rolls thank you. But what about her protein, you will ask — no worries, she's only eating one meal at your house, she already got her daily protein (see above).

4. **Do not say "You don't eat meat? Not even chicken?"**: Really people, this one is pretty simple — she does not eat animals. Yes, fish and chicken are animals. If you TRULY don't get this one, a basic biology class may be in order.

5. **Do not try to convert her back**: She will not give YOU a lecture for eating meat (though she could) so do not give her one for abstaining.

Well, there you have it — the basics on how to politely communicate with a vegetarian. She is a friend to all animals, healthier than us, and a better steward of the earth's resources (the quantity of grain and water needed to raise one cow is crazy).

So if you sit next to a vegetarian on Thursday, instead of rolling your eyes or asking "Why?" just smile and say, "Good for you! and HAPPY THANKSGIVING TO US ALL!!"

FREE THE PRESIDENTIAL APOSTROPHE

This year for the first time I realized that no one can agree on where to place the apostrophe (if at all) in President's' Day. A quick search on the internet shows that the definitive answer is obvious — call it Washington's Birthday.

But since I saw it in commercials for mattresses spelled three different ways I was compelled to figure out which way is correct.

Digression: Why mattresses and presidents? (though JFK and Clinton come to mind when searching for a connection). Can you imagine George saying to Martha, "Some day I hope they commemorate me and all the great men and women *(in this Downton Abbey-like revisionist version I am making him a feminist)* who hold my job in the future by offering great deals on mattresses!!"

No of course not. He would have wanted the day commemorated by giving our kids the day off of school so we can take them to Nickel City (local arcade) which, at this time of year, as my neighbor Danielle pointed out, could also be called Cesspool.

Or we could honor them by cramming the day full of orthodontist appointments and last-minute rehearsals for the high-school variety show. Whatever.

Back to the apostrophe. I am going to make a case here.

It can't be President's Day because that would imply we are only honoring one president which defeats the whole purpose of changing it from Washington's Birthday in the first place.

It technically could be Presidents' Day for obvious reasons.

But this year I noticed a lot of companies went with the somewhat confusing Presidents Day. I had this explained to me once by a colleague, Mary Brent who pointed out that if you use a noun enough it kind of becomes an adjective and you don't need to worry about possession anymore. Her example was Farmers Insurance.

I also noticed that Sears and BMW went apostrophe-free (in their TV ads anyway) and I choose to believe they have some of the best copywriters left in the world.

Tweeters don't do copy-writing so maybe I need to explain....Well kids, once upon a time there were people who, never mind. It gives me comfort to imagine a room full of smart English majors debating this over at Sears headquarters. Sears' headquarters. Errr...

So I make the case to go apostrophe-free. I have at least two regular readers who are English majors (Amy and Lorri) who may want to thrust and parry on this. Go for it.

And while I am suggesting we let go of that apostrophe, and we are fresh off the Family Christmas Card Season, a gentle reminder that you should not sign the card "Love, the Brown's" It is simply, "Love, the Browns".

Think about it a minute, I'll wait.

Oh, no, I do not think you are a silly goose for making this very common mistake and did it myself for MANY years. But stop it now.

So today's lesson is that with apostrophes, as with mattress sales, less is more and if I ever figure out commas I can share that with you too.

THAT DRAWER AND BAND POLOS

Now that we are hip deep in the electronic age pretty much every house has "That drawer". You know the one. The one where old (and current) chargers go to die. If you have a few cell phones, laptops, and digital cameras in your house you have a bunch of these cords in a tangle somewhere. Add to the mess that the teens in your house upgrade their phones every few years so you have the old ones in there too. Add a husband who has just moved from a Blackberry to an iPhone and now you have even more.

This drawer makes you crazy. Every time you go to look for your own phone charger (for the oldest phone in the house—somehow you always have the oldest phone in the house) you paw through the mess and think, "Can't someone come up with a better way to store these?"

You might even try a charging station but this will not work at all. Why? Because even if you make a nice little spot to charge things your children will still insist on charging their phones all over the house. So you will give up and go back to the drawer.

One day, you will have had enough and in a rare moment when all the kids are home at once, you pull out the mess of cords and hold each one up saying, "How about this? Does this belong to any of you?" and they will clutch their own chargers to their breasts and say , "No. It's not mine," and you, who have just set aside your own phone and camera chargers and your husband's new phone charger, will with great confidence and a feeling of accomplishment, toss the old stuff in the garbage. You have a tiny twinge of guilt because you are pretty sure you are supposed to recycle old chargers but really, sometimes you just say "screw it" and throw things away willy-nilly and irresponsibly (the latest earth infraction you have been committing without even knowing it is batteries—who knew you were supposed to 'dispose of them responsibly'? and how would one do that?) But I digress...

Now you have a clean and orderly drawer and you actually know what device belongs to each and every cord in the house and you are proud and feel clean and good and righteous.

Until.

Until that morning when you are all rushing around to get out the door and your husband who is not usually part of this mix but is today because he has to fly to Nashville to make a presentation, says to the room at large, "Has anyone seen my laptop charger?"

You look up from putting your flip-flops on in preparation of driving the second shift of kids to school and gauge the crowd. Should you confess at once or play dumb and pray the teens who are stuffing their backpacks and slipping into their hoodies do not give you up. After a moment you see they are not taking the bait. They are good children and would not shout out "Mom threw a bunch of those away." No. They know this will result in a scene and a scene could make them late for school. So they stay loyally mum for mum, so to speak.

Out of sheer desperation you go upstairs and rummage through some silly bag of parts you once bought called an "iGo" and you try to plug nibs into your husband's laptop and though you find one that fits you cannot find the other end that should plug into the wall. Still, you try to sell this device to your husband. "Here is something that fits! Perhaps you could get the rest of this at the airport!" But by now he is in no mood and as he approaches a melt-down you make your escape shouting, "Gotta take the kids to school!"

As you drive the kids to school, leaving him to search through the house for his charger that you are fairly certain you threw away, you come up with a dozen reasons why this is not your fault. It's not like you went into his laptop bag and took the charger and threw it away. No. He must have left it out for weeks for it to have ended up in "the drawer." This is what he gets for being so careless. As you drive back from school you hope desperately that the cab will have come and taken this problem, I mean , your husband to the airport.

But alas, the cab is just arriving when you pull in the driveway and you steel yourself to go in and confess and try to help the man you love, the man who supports you all, find his stupid laptop charger because really, without it he cannot make a presentation to new clients in Nashville, and he will not get paid, and you will all starve and it will be your fault because you just had to clean "the drawer."

However, much to your surprise, when you go in the house your husband is smiling. He found his charger and in fact is rather sheepish about it because he found it under a pile of crap on his own dresser and you are too relieved to give him a hard time about it. And you don't have to because he laughs and says, "My god, I'm as bad as the kids when they wait until about 10 minutes before the band concert to realize they don't have black pants that fit and their band polo is in the laundry," and you resist the temptation to say, "Yes, exactly," because you know this could have turned out very badly for you like the unfortunate knife-drawer purge of 2008 which still comes up from time to time.

And as you kiss him goodbye and send him on his way, you wonder what the moral of this story is — is it that you should not throw away old electronic stuff? is it that no matter what happens at home it is mom's fault? or could it just be that the other people in your house need to keep track of their shit a little better?

Nah, now that's just crazy talk.

THE ROYAL WEDDING: THEN AND NOW

Ever since it was announced that Prince William will be marrying this spring, those of us of a certain age cannot help but reminisce about when our Princess Di got married. We can't help it, it was such a wonderful, beautiful fairy-tale wedding. And we can't help but compare that wedding to this wedding. Here are some of my observations:

That Princess: I loved Diana. She was so sweet, so charming, so my age. She worked for a living even though she came from some distant royally connected family. She was shy and kept her chin down. She had short, sassy hair.

This Princess: I don't know why and it is not fair to say this, but I don't love Kate. I think it's because she is (like most girls in the media these days) just a little too slick. She would never be caught wearing a see-through floral skirt with the sun behind her. Her teeth are perfect. Her makeup is too. She is a party girl and I just cannot imagine our Princess Di throwing back tequila shots (well, not in her twenties...she did that later). Kate was working, sort of, for her family's business —a party supply company— which is just not as noble as taking care of little children. And, (now this is just catty), she has no upper lip. She has predictable hair.

That Prince: Charles was a douche. Even then we were pretty sure he did not really love Diana. He married her because his mum told him it was time to marry someone and Di happened to be the virgin standing in front of him when the music stopped in the game of musical-chairs-date-a-prince game. In his defense he was never parented very well. But still, he should have manned up and told his mum he'd get married when he fell in love.

This Prince: I like the boy. He is darling and was so brave when his mum died. He was loved by his mom and that goes a long way toward making a man who can love properly. He does stuff that shows he understands the gravity of his inherited role and also the importance of appearing a little less ostentatious—for example his choice to maintain a home without servants. It's cute. Not the smartest thing but cute.

The virgin thing then: Doctors had to examine Princess Diana to verify that she was a virgin before she could marry Charles (who was notoriously not a virgin). WTF? No one knew why really—I mean it wasn't a hundred years ago, just 30, and everyone was having a lot of sex. But for some reason, poor Diana was expected not to have and was subjected to this humiliation. It was implied that it was just a rule and there was nothing anyone could do about it.

The virgin thing now: Apparently it is no longer a requirement which means someone could have done something about this requirement 30 years ago. This is irritating —not because I think Kate should be a virgin but for the implied fact that someone (the Queen?) could have dropped this qualification back in 1981 and saved us all a lot of trouble (not to mention Diana's life). Old Chuck could have married the icky love of his life and Diana would have been free to marry a commoner and live a nice long life with a man who actually loved her. Now that would have been a fairy-tale ending.

The ride to the church then: Was that not the best part of the whole damn day? Watching our bee-yoo-tiful princess in the glass-covered horse-drawn carriage as she rode to Westminster Abbey? I loved that part.

The ride to the church now: Kate is taking a car. Not sure why. According to the Huffington Post, William wanted to save money but the Queen pointed out that the whole Royal Guard will be on hand that day anyway so there's no savings. Then someone said maybe security but no, the bride and groom will be going in an open horse and carriage after the wedding. So who knows. All I know is that I agree with Grace who said, "Not going in the glass-covered coach!!! That's the whole reason you marry a prince!" Exactly.

And finally:

The marriage then: Well, unfortunately it was a sham. A farce and a myth. We kind of knew that going into it (as did Diana) but we really, really hoped for the best(as did Diana). But it was not to be.

The marriage now: It looks like the real deal. Kate and Will are good friends and have known each other for years. No one pushed them into this. It would be lovely if we could get a royal who could stay happily married. It's been a while since that's happened. So I wish those two crazy kids all the luck in the world.

And I know our Princess will be smiling down on their special day, wishing the same thing for her little boy.

iPad myPad

If there's one thing I can do well it is pontificate and pronounce. No, wait, that's two things. Well, I do them a lot. I think of a brilliant idea, or notion, or theory and I turn it around in my head and then I pronounce. Prompted by a mere nod of your head I will go on (and on just a bit). I will polish the hypothesis then tell it afresh to someone else and someone else and someone else and unfortunately to you again (oops sorry). I'm especially insightful and eloquent if I've had a martini or two (and prone to tell an old theory again).

I have lots of theories that I hold on to tightly some times for years. Most of you have heard them. Many times. I hold on tight right until I don't. And then I've been known to drop the theory, take the opposite side and argue for it just as vehemently. But I can't think of any of these golden nuggets I have ever dropped as quickly as I did on Christmas day.

So here's my original gem (as if you haven't heard it): On newspapers in print vs. electronic form: Ahem. I know it makes more sense to get your morning news on a computer and I see that my kids are pretty comfortable with that. And I know that the day is fast approaching when papers will not be printed. But electronic news is not for me. No sirree. I LOVE having my New York Times at the end of the driveway. I LOVE hearing it hit the driveway with a thump then go out in my bathrobe (no coat, year round, that is my rule, no matter how cold) and then come back to the counter and unsheathe it and dive in, coffee cup in hand. That's right. That's how I've always done it and that's how I'll always do it. Go ahead younger folk, kids, and early adapters—feel free to get your news on your silly Smart Phone or you goofy iPhone or your little laptop or whatever. But I will be sticking to the old newsprint. That's just the way I roll. I'm old school and proud of it. I love my print paper and I am so grateful for those who print it and deliver it to me every day.

Then on Christmas morning Jeff gave me an iPad. An iPad! I never even dreamed of having one. I mean it's cool but I'm the last one in the house to get anything electronically cool. I have a cell phone that's two-kids old (moms will know what that means) and I can't even figure out how to text properly on it. But there it was, under the tree—an iPad! In about ten minutes I had that puppy up and running and sliding my hand across it in that satisfying way they show on the commercial, making stuff bigger then smaller with magic spider fingers. Soon I was surfing Facebook from the couch (oh, THAT's how you get addicted to Facebook)

After a while we moved the post-unwrapping party into the kitchen for coffee and newspaper time. Jeff volunteered to shovel out to get the paper for me. While he was gone I leaned over, hit about three different buttons on my iPad and downloaded the free New York Times app. By the time he brought that stupid, enormous, environmentally unsound hunk of tree-pulp covered in snow behemoth to the counter I was already reading the front page in vivid color, in print big enough for my aging eyes, with that nice back light, on my nice little lightweight iPad.

I sipped my coffee and looked up at Jeff, as if I were surprised he'd bothered to get that relic from last century at all—"Thanks for getting that but I probably don' t need it now." In less than five minutes I'd converted. And the only thing it took for me to do this was to —wait for it—actually TRY it.

I then went on to enjoy my Sunday Times in a whole new way. I read entire articles because I wasn't flipping through pages, getting distracted and forgetting what page the story was continued on (whoever started that stupid custom?). I downloaded the crossword puzzle app and discovered the beauty of that (oh yeah, crossworders—you want to do this, believe me).

And there you have it. I don't want to cancel my print subscription just yet. I'd feel bad for Wayne, my paper deliveryman who I just tipped for the holidays. And the nice thing about the print version is you can share the paper. The kids do still look it over from time to time. Right after they check the news on the internet. I probably will keep getting the print version until I can figure out how my iPad can make a nice satisfying thump on the driveway. Maybe Jeff could set it out there for me and I could go get it in my bathrobe.

Whatever I decide at least you no longer have to hear me go on about why I prefer print to electronic newspapers.

Unfortunately, you're going to have to hear about how great my new iPad is.

FACEBOOK: TIDAL WAVE

I suppose earlier generations had to sit through all this huffing and puffing with the invention of television, the phone, cinema, radio, the car, the bicycle, printing, the wheel and so on, but you would think we would learn the way these things work, which is this:
1) everything that's already in the world when you're born is just normal;
2) anything that gets invented between then and before you turn thirty is incredibly exciting and creative and with any luck you can make a career out of it;
3) anything that gets invented after you're thirty is against the natural order of things and the beginning of the end of civilization as we know it until it's been around for about ten years when it gradually turns out to be alright really.

—Douglas Adams, Sunday Times, August 29, 1999

So, are you on Facebook? Probably. Now that Facebook membership is up to 500 million (that would be 200 million more than the population of this country) you have probably jumped on board. I did a while back and since I've been on for more than a year I'd like to make a few observations.

1. If you are not on Facebook, do not brag about it: Yes, we know, you don't get it. You say you don't need to know that your best friend from high school is making pot-roast. Saying that is the equivalent of saying,

"Airplanes! If God wanted me to fly he would have given me wings!" To quote Bob Dylan, "*Come mothers and fathers Throughout the land And don't criticize What you can't understand Your sons and your daughters Are beyond your command*" Besides, when you say stuff like that, it makes you sound, well, old.

If you are new to Facebook—here are some tips:

2. Do not take quizzes or answer questions that your friends "send" you: I do not understand how this all works but if you answer a simple question or take a fun quiz, Facebook sends weird messages to all your friends and you may not even know it. This happened to my friend Mary who answered something silly and next thing she knew, all her friends received an alleged messaged from her asking if they thought Jack M. had a nice ass. This is especially weird because Jack M. is her son. Eww.

3. Don't play Farmville: This is apparently an addictive game you can play on Facebook and I'm sure it is quite fun. I myself like to waste time doing crossword puzzles so who am I to say Farmville is or is not a good way to pass the time. But the thing is when you play Farmville, Facebook sends out messages, unbeknownst to you, broadcasting messages like "Cindy needs just one more plank to build her pigpen!" Which is just another way of saying "Cindy is playing Farmville at work again!" Thank goodness my crossword puzzle does not do this to me or you would learn just how much time I spent trying to figure out a five-letter word for Caribbean getaway when I was supposed to be doing the laundry.

4. Never respond to a post truthfully or sarcastically—it's not the Facebook way: Since everyone on Facebook is a friend, the tone is quite kind and civil (I'm speaking of adults here, apparently the under 20-set can get ugly). This means when someone from your past posts "Just got back from the mall! So happy to find a lot of clothes in size 0 and 2!", you should not respond with, "Who in the hell were you shopping for?" or even the obvious, "Bitch." Instead you must say something like, "OMG, you're so skinny still!" and "You have such a darling figure, I'm so jealous!!!!!"

And, along the same vein, when people post photos you must always tell them how darling they/their pet/their children are. And they really are because no one posts bad pictures of themselves and if their kids are ugly they don't post those pictures either.

So that's what I know so far. Facebook is a fact of life for better or for worse and it's not going anywhere soon. It's a great way for people of a certain age to keep in touch with the friends, coworkers, and relatives you tend to acquire from a life well-lived. And yes, I do want to know that today is Val's birthday, and Christine is on her way to California, and Wendy had a killer margarita in Mexico City last night. These things make me smile.

If I figure out Twitter, I'll let you know.

FACEBOOK: GO AHEAD TRY IT

Sometimes I find myself defending Facebook to those who haven't tried it. Invariably these people tell me it's a waste of time and they don't care if their friend is making baked chicken and rice pilaf for dinner. I understand their sentiments; I felt the same way a year ago. But that was before I joined the 70 billion other people on Facebook.

My Facebook habit started like most habits do. I 'only' signed up because I was trying to find a particular person, Wendy, who had been in Spain with me in the early 80's. I was hoping to organize a reunion for the seven or eight of us who shared that seminal time. The reunion never came to pass but I did find Wendy who now lives in Mexico married to the very boy she was dating all those years ago. I was delighted to reconnect with her if only in this little way.

As soon as I signed up I felt the heady rush of popularity as 'friend requests' poured in. All these people I know want to be my friend? Little old me? Of course now I realize that Facebook is set up so cleverly that people might be asking you to be their friend almost by accident. It combs email addresses and school affiliated lists to show you names of people you might know and might want to friend. Then, if you just twitch your finger near the enter button it shoots invitations out to them all.

But I didn't know that. I was flattered to be asked to be a friend. Yes! I will be your friend, I responded and so I jumped in. I didn't want to get "hooked" on Facebook of course, so I set up a policy for myself, 'I will only friend people on Facebook if they ask me first.' This is a little like saying, 'I will only eat the folded potato chips' to limit calories. It is a false and useless control system.

For a while I coasted by with that, only visiting Facebook if someone spoke to me directly (these messages come in to your email). Then I saw Richard B.'s name on someone else's friend list and I broke my first rule. Richard! I loved Richard! He was an old high school/band buddy who I'd completely lost touch with and I would love to know where he was and what he was up to. I friended him.

Now the floodgates were open. What happened to that woman whose wedding we went to in the eighties but had abruptly stopped getting Christmas cards from in the 90s? Want to know? Friend her! I started dreaming about people from my past. The neighbors we lived next door to for only one year in 1968. What were their names? There were seven kids and I played with Annette and my brother played with Ricky. Wonder what they're doing now? Look for them on Facebook! And Patti H. I was her BFF for one month in 1977 when we traveled to Spain with the Spanish club. She was from Pittsburgh; I from Detroit but we were pen pals for years. Whatever happened to her? Facebook her!

And so, like so many other people I am a bit of a fan of Facebook. After making fun of social media like the old cranky person I am, I am now a convert. I am not alone. According to Facebook the majority of their users are over 50 and that does not surprise me a bit. How else can you accumulate several dozen friends over the years unless you've lived several decades? And it is great for keeping in touch with all those people with whom you once had relationships in your storied past—from a co-worker at your first job to the kid you back-packed through Europe with—maybe you don't keep in touch by mail or phone but that doesn't mean they are forgotten.

That's the great thing about Facebook—just like email keeps us in touch in ways we would never have thought possible (my 10-year-old emails her 94-year-old Great Grandma) so does Facebook. So yes, you nay-sayers, it is a bit of a time waster but I do indeed want to know that Wendy had fabulous salsa last week and Cher is thankful for the sunny day and Barb made a memorial rock garden for her sister this weekend.

In this tiny way I get to stay connected to all the people who were ever dear to me on a weekly basis not just through the dreary custom of Christmas cards (oh holiday letters, that's an entirely different blog). And in a world that moves ever faster I find that immensely comforting.

By the way, in case you were wondering, I'm making baked chicken and rice pilaf for dinner.

PAPER OR PLASTIC

I just came from Whole Foods and I thought I'd get some swordfish because everyone knows we should get more Omega-3 oils in our diet. The only thing was I couldn't remember what kind to buy. As I stood at the counter trying to remember if I'm supposed to buy fresh or farmed (something about mercury?) Alaskan or Norwegian (something about over-harvesting?) I noticed a sign that said "Harpoon-caught Swordfish" Under those words, in small print, I was informed that it was "from a fishery certified sustainable by the Marine Stewardship Council."

Now first of all I have to take exception with the phrase, "Harpoon-caught". I'm pretty sure "harpoon-impaled" or just plain old "harpooned" would be more accurate but then that doesn't sound so nice does it?Harpoon-caught. Okay, sure, that must be a good thing or why else would they put it on the sign? No nets to accidentally catch dolphins or something. But wait a minute—what exactly are the harpoons made of? What if they're made of teak and come from a rain forest (formerly known as a "jungle") and each time you eat a fish that has been harpooned a teak tree is cut down to make the harpoon and the beautiful rain forest is being destroyed which in turn leads to increased global warming and those melting ice caps so the penguins, like the ones in that cute movie no longer have a place to live (although I saw how cold they are and it wouldn't hurt them to warm up just a teeny bit). Anyhoo, do I really want the deforestation of yet another rain forest on my conscience? No. No I just could not support harpoon-caught salmon without further research.

So I went off to the vitamin aisle in search of fish oil supplements for my Omega-3's but then I remembered I read something about being careful of which kind of fish oil to buy because, well, I don't remember why. Something about how the fish oil is harvested—sometimes it is cruel or "unsustainable" (formerly known as "wasteful"). Think about it—how DO they get all that fish oil? Milk them? Wring them out then throw them back? The truth is I had no idea and now I felt like just another thoughtless, lazy consumer who might as well be buying McDonald's cruelly-raised food and taking it home in a non-biodegradable plastic bag and giving my kids the Happy Toy made by a child-slave in China. So I nixed the fish oil.

I veered away from the vitamin aisle and realized I still needed something for dinner so went back to the meat counter. I decided to get burger, (Lilly could eat a veggie burger). I read the choices carefully and after convincing myself that the cattle had been raised humanely, in sunshine, allowed to eat real grass, not fed hormones or antibiotics, AND that no workers were exploited, the neighbors were not offended by the smell of the cattle ranch, and that no American lost his job in the process, I went ahead and bought a pound. Exhausted, I stumbled to the checkout counter only to realize I had left my reusable bag in the car. I felt too guilty to use a paper bag for just a pound of beef so I put it in my purse and left quietly, thinking wistfully of a time when our mothers' only tough choice to make at the A&P was beef, chicken, or pork.

LOVE NOTES IN LUNCH BAGS

"So here I am, up to my ass in papers; permission slips, assignment notebooks, reading logs—I'm making eggs for four kids AND I'm packing four lunches," Coffee Friend 2 is describing her morning,"and BOOM Izzy says it, '*Mooooommmmm*, why don't you ever put a note in my lunch like Morgan's mom does?" Coffee Friend 2 looks at me for emphasis, "Can you f**ing believe it? A note. In her goddamn lunch. Like I got time for this shit!"

Her youngest, the five-year-old interjects here, "Mom, I can hear you." Coffee Friend 2 shrugs apologetically.

Sigh. My friend has just fallen victim to the hyper-mom-syndrome. This is what happens when you take a bunch of lawyers and MBAs and they decide to stay home with their kids full time. They take all that go-go-go energy, all that extra-credit and over-time mentality that worked so well for them in college and the career world and apply it to their parenting which really requires a different skill set altogether with the first skill being, reeelaaaxxxx.

It is not enough that they offer their kids every opportunity at every sport and artistic endeavor available. It is not enough that they sit behind me at a restaurant and make Tyler do his multiplication tables while they wait for their macrobiotic meal (mine are coloring and eating mac and cheese). It is not enough that they volunteer for every activity at school and are on every PTA-type board (which reminds me of the recently-stay-at-home bank VP who used to say "vis-a-vis" at nursery school board meetings until I once broke out into a fit of giggles—I mean really we were discussing who would bring the lemonade and she somehow worked "vis-a-vis" into the sentence). No on top of it all they must put love notes into their kids' little lunches.

And that would be all well and good if our own children would just stop looking around and noticing we do not do some of this nicey nice stuff. Who needs that? I'm still recovering from a sleep over that Lilly went to hosted by the nicest mom in the world, Khaki Voss (the same one who has a Christmas party the night of ours and siphons our friends away—she and I are going to have to have a throw down in aisle 4 of the Dominick's if this keeps up). Apparently, Khaki—known as "Ella's Mom" in this story, not only stays up late to check on the girls at sleep overs and offer them timely snacks (I close the basement door and go to bed at 9:00) but she gets up early and makes the girls pancakes! In cute animal shapes! Damn you Khaki Voss and your Mickey Mouse shaped pancakes!

"Do you put notes in the kids' lunches?" CF2 asks me at the end of her rant.

After I finish snorting hot coffee out my nose I answer, "What lunches? They make their own. Actually, Lilly once wrote herself a note and asked me to sign it. Is that wrong?"

CF2 looked relieved. I know how she feels. Sometimes it feels like you're Alice in Wonderland and you're not sure if you're crazy or everyone else is. A wise social worker once told me it's important to seek out parents who share your parenting values so you don't start doubting everything you do.

Which is why I have coffee with that wise social worker once a week. And neither of us puts love notes in our kids lunches every day.

A LOVE STORY FOR VALENTINE'S DAY

Mary grew up in Western Michigan in a small rural town outside of Grand Rapids. Unlike her other siblings (all of whom still live in her hometown) she was subject to wanderlust and managed to get herself to Paris and then Madrid her junior year and that's where I met her — in Madrid. We were instant companions and I was drawn to her dry sense of humor (drier than mine even) and her shocking way of saying exactly what is on her mind to almost anyone at any time. We palled around Madrid that spring, drinking too much beer and following the cast of Conan the Barbarian to parties.

She ended up back in Michigan (as did I for a time) and we've kept in touch over the years. She got married young, had two boys young, and got divorced young. Since her divorce many years ago she has dated off and on but she seems to attract highly undesirable men and her Christmas cards are often filled with hilarious accounts of these men like the monk who liked to be spanked and the DJ who asked her to, well, I can't say what he asked her to do but she politely declined, and the blind date who was wearing tinfoil on his head so he wouldn't hear the voices. She teaches speech therapy (or something like that, she's going to correct me now) for the Flint school district which is as close to working for the Peace Corps as a paid position can be.

In all these years she has never gotten back to Europe. In all these years, she has pretty much given up on finding a nice man to spend her life with.

Laurent is my Dutch friend. I met him in 1986 when he opened the door to the communal dorm kitchen in Eindhoven, The Netherlands to find me standing there blinking in the bright Dutch sun of a June day, jet-lagged, and a little confused having arrived for an internship without anyone to greet me at the airport. I had somehow made my way to the dorm I was to stay in but no one seemed to know I was coming. He smiled and invited me in for tea and cookies. We have been friends ever since. We kept in touch by letters and then the internet. He is passionate about old cars and guitars. He knows more about anything than anyone I know in the world. He speaks Dutch (of course) and English fluently. He is also quite fluent in German and French though he downplays this. He has had little experience with the opposite sex and often wonders about this. As he says, "Charles Manson gets marriage proposals. How is it I can't find a nice girl?" Exactly. I've encouraged him to internet date but that too has had its share of disappointments. He has long ago given up on the idea of finding a nice girl to share his life with.

Then last June I noticed that the two most frequent posters on this blog were Mary and Laurent. I realized they had a lot in common: they are both socialists, they both are very interested in everyone and everything around them, they are both extremely outspoken, frank, and honest, and they are both among the kindest people I know. I knew they would have fun "talking" on the internet and I introduced them to each other then left them to chat in the corner with a drink in each hand (metaphorically speaking—this was all by internet).

A few months later Mary revealed that she really, really liked Laurent but wondered how far things could progress being an ocean apart. I urged Mary to beg, borrow, and steal money to go see Laurent.

So for the first time in nearly 30 years, Mary got out her passport and took a plane across the Atlantic.

The trip was such a success that Laurent is now visiting Mary in Michigan (in February—think about that).

They are both coming to visit us this weekend. Mary apologized for "intruding" on Valentine's Day weekend but really, can you think of anything more romantic than sharing dinner with a couple involved in an overseas romance on Valentine's Day?

Me neither! Happy Valentine's Day everyone and remember love really does come along when you least expect it.

I'VE GOT GUYS

When you move to your first house after living in dorms and apartments and condos you quickly learn that no landlord or association is going to fix your house stuff—it's up to you. There are problems with any house: refrigerators break; chimneys get clogged; toilets leak; hot water heaters stop working and you don't know a whole lot about how to fix them so you need reliable help. After a few years of that, you may move on to the home-improvement phase of home ownership and then you realize there are even more things you don't know like how to build a fence; design a brick patio; or the big kahuna—put an addition on.

You need help. You need professionals to come do stuff for you and you learn quickly that it is not a good idea to randomly choose someone from the phone book or the internet. No, like dating, it is much better to get a recommendation instead of going into it blindly. So you will soon find yourself asking all your friends "do you have a guy for_____" fill in the blank: painting, plumbing, HVAC, taxes etc. That's how I have found almost all my guys—from friends recommending them.

I have always found wonderful people this way. Like marriage, when you find the right guy, it is a thing of beauty. A serendipitous thing that brings to your life so much more than someone to fix something. In it's best form you will find someone who enriches your life and leaves you better for having known him.

So here, I pay tribute to some of my most memorable guys.

Richard: Richard was truly my first guy. A handyman who worked for the village by day and fixed everything in the neighborhood by night. When I called him to replace my bathroom door which had a split right down the middle he declared it was too fine of a door to replace. Instead, he took it home and glued it with boat glue and charged me a fraction of the cost of a new door. He did a lot more around the house and then he disappeared. Phone disconnected and everything. I suspect he really did retire to Florida (even though he was only 35) as he often threatened to do on the money he made off of all of us (every penny earned). A good handyman is almost impossible to find, even one you've used before.

Sean: Sean came to paint the outside of our brick house one spring. He only worked when the conditions were perfect so he wasn't there every day and he was meticulous. He did not even start painting until Fourth of July because he had spent a month scraping the old paint off first. He took the shutters down, primed them, put them back to cure for two weeks, then took them down and painted them again. He was Irish, still had his brogue, and said "shite" for "shit" which slayed me. He was a former trader who wanted to stay home to keep an eye on his youngest who was an adult but mentally challenged. She had had leukemia in the seventies and was cured but given so much radiation it had affected her mind. He would paint and then get a call from his wife asking for help with her and off he'd go. I didn't mind one bit. He did not finish the job until Halloween but he charged me just a fraction of what the others had bid the job at. That paint job has lasted more than ten years. He told me he really only worked for something to do and if someone asked him to bid on a job and he didn't like the people he just gave them a ridiculous quote to get rid of them. He was a wonderful man and I hope he is still around enjoying his family.

Duncan: Duncan is a landscape designer and the person who gave me his name described him as a genius who looks like a dirty Santa. This is true. White hair and beard, ample belly, and dirt under his nails because he does his own planting. I had contacted him once but he didn't seem in any hurry to do the job. Then one Saturday, without warning, he appeared in the back yard and asked if he could sit and draw up some plans. He got a card table and chair from his truck then set up in back with paper and pencil. He asked me questions like "How do you use this space?" "What feeling do you want to convey?" He told me I didn't really want a pergola (I had been quite sure I had) over the patio because it would make the back too busy with too much going on. What was the pergola for? Shade? Then he'd get me a nice shade tree. While talking to him about family I learned he was the father of 10 children. His wife had died years before and he was raising them alone. I commented that it must be hard and sad. "Not really, she was more needed with God then she was here. We'll be together again some day," he said with true conviction. I also learned that his oldest son was a Wilms Tumor survivor—the same kidney cancer that Lilly had. My Belief that these wonderful men are not sent to me randomly grows. By the way, the shade tree is gorgeous and the pergola really would have been too much.

Andreas: Andreas is my yard guy. He came to me a few years back when I realized Jeff and I had completely given up any notion of taking care of our own yard and it was starting to be an embarrassment. He cleaned up a year's worth of overgrowth and neglect in two days. The next week I asked how much to move two small trees for me. "$150" he said. Later he came with his helper and they dug up the trees in the pouring rain, transplanting them and their sizable root balls by hand with a wheelbarrow. When he came to the door, soaking wet, he said, "That didn't take as long as I thought, I will only charge you $100." Seriously. I had to beg him to take the full amount. Then last winter I called him to see if he could get some ice out of my gutters. He went up on the roof and shoveled it all while his nervous looking helper held the ladder. He did that for over an hour (it was about 6 degrees that day)then came to the door. "I couldn't get the ice off so I really can't charge you anything." Seriously. I had to beg him to take $20 for shoveling my roof. I have to mention that Andreas is from Mexico so I doubt shoveling roofs is something he's terribly comfortable doing but he tried because I asked him.

Michael: Well you all know about Michael. He's my nearly mythical contractor that put the addition on for us six years ago. He comes back a lot to do odd jobs for me. Right now he's downstairs walling up a doorway I've always hated. He's a little like Eldon from Murphy Brown if you remember that character. The kids just say good morning over their eggs like he lives here when he lets himself in. I think maybe I've grown a little too accustomed to having him here because yesterday, after we conducted a brief meeting about the aforementioned door opening, I realized I was still in my pajamas.

So those are some of the guys in my life. Just a small listing really. I didn't even tell you about Painter Dude or Tile Guy or my accountant Bob who made that problem with the IRS go away in about ten minutes or Joe who invests our money more cautiously than I would. When Lilly was sick Joe and Bob (who do not even know each other) pretty much did my taxes for me that year. I love them all and thank the universe for bringing them into our house and our lives. May God bless you with some great guys too.

MORE OF WHAT PASSES FOR CONVERSATION AROUND HERE

Summer School

This spring Atticus(15) asked us if he could take a summer school class. That's what the kids do around here—not so often to make up a bad grade but to get a class out of the way and have some breathing room during the school year. We were opposed to the idea. "You're only young once, why do you want to spoil it with school?" we asked him." Think of all that down time you're giving up." But he was not to be dissuaded.

"Please, Mom and Dad, let me take chemistry," he actually begged. At last we relented and I signed him up for two summer semesters. Having allowed him to take this class (and paid for it) we wanted to impress upon him that he needed to take it seriously and get a decent grade. But we did not want to say "You must get an 'A'" or anything that definitive because as any parent knows you only cause trouble for yourself if you go around making such quantifiable demands. So Jeff tried a casual approach.

"You know, if you're going to take that class we want you to apply yourself."

"Yeah, I know," Atticus grunted.

"So you should, you know, stay out of the 'C-hood'," Jeff said and warming to his clever use of language pushed on, "And kind of shoot for at least the 'B-ville'," and now thinking he was handling this just right, "And really, we'd like you to keep it in the 'A-ness'."

At which point he had to stop talking because all three kids and I were laughing so hard he couldn't continue.

My T-shirt

So I like to wear my Obama t-shirt as a pajama top. It has his head and shoulders and the words "Obama 2008" on it. Because it is my pajama top, I do not wear undergarments with it.

One morning, as I sat in my Obama pajama top reading the New York Times, Lilly came in and got herself a bowl of cereal. After several minutes of silence she looked up at me and in a pretty spot-on imitation of our president said, "Look, umm, I'm just saying, if you are going to wear that and your breasts are resting on my shoulders, umm, you should at least think about wearing a bra and bring those things up to my ears."

BATHROOM REMODEL

The girls' bathroom is the only original room in this house. It still has hideous peachy-orange tile with black trim. Apparently that was in style when the house was built in 1947. When we first moved in I replaced the vanity (I did that myself I might add and will NEVER attempt a do-it-yourself plumbing project again. There's a reason plumbers make so much money) but even that was a decade ago and it is looking sad. Then there was the leak. Michael gave me the bad news last month — the clamp he put on the leaking pipe which is in the floor of the bathroom/ceiling of the downstairs — was only temporary and about the only way to get at it is to pull out the old tub. Might as well re-do the whole bath.

To my surprise Jeff agreed. "Absolutely. That bathroom is hideous." And so it was decided.

Since Grace is the one who spends the most time in there I enlisted her help. She immediately got out her colored pencils and drew up three different plans of where the new vanity would go, how many new jets would be on the new shower, and what the tile would look like.

Unfortunately for Grace the bathroom is only 8' x6' (hard to believe it was the only full bath for the first 50 years this house existed and I know for a fact there were four boys living here in the 70s) and Michael informed me there really is no way to move anything anywhere nor is there room to expand anything. After the time she spent drawing up the elaborate plans we can't use she was exceedingly disappointed. So I told her she could choose the new vanity.

After an extensive internet search she chose one of those things that looks like a bowl set on top of a dresser. This is progress? This is what our great-grandparents washed up with—but I know they are in style right now. "Umm, Grace, I don't know if this is practical," I cautioned. "It will be hard to clean and also it's too trendy."

"TOO trendy?" she blinked. "Isn't trendy a good thing?"

"Oh right. Usually but you know, it will be really outdated in ten years or so."

"Ten years?" she blinked again. She's a very expressive blinker. I may as well have said a hundred years. What is ten years to a 14 year old? More than half her life that's what. Sometimes she doesn't understand me at all. I thought about it. Why on earth would she care if our bathroom looks dated in ten years? In ten years she'll be in her first apartment in LA waiting tables at night and going to auditions in the day. (A side-note here about how quickly time passes when you're old—I know, a recurring theme for me—last week I was making chili and I thought, "Hmm, this chili powder is probably a few years old now because my ex-sister-in-law bought it for me and they've already been divorced two years, so I checked the expiration date: 1995. The kids were howling at me.)

Anyhoo, sometimes I have to remind myself that one of the bad things about getting older, wiser, and more practical is that if you're not careful you can end up with a suitable, non-trendy bathroom that won't go out of style for twenty years (and 15 year old chili powder). It's nice to have kids around to remind you of that (and laugh at your old spices).

So after more thought I'm ditching my practical approach. Next time you're over make sure I show you our new bathroom. It will be trendy and look great.

But look quick — it will be out of style by 2020.

Afterwards, we'll have some bland chili.

OUT OF THE WOODS

Okay, you know the self-righteous housewife doesn't often wade into the world of pop culture, as I leave that to the experts at People and Perez Hilton but this Tiger Woods story is too good for me to pass on. So here it goes:

There are so many weird pieces of the story we know (the story we don't know is probably sadly familiar) that I just have to comment on a few of them.

Point One: Rich and famous people don't know their neighbors: As pointed out by my son, how is it that Tiger Woods' neighbor did not know that was him lying outside his car? I mean, in my neighborhood, if Tiger Woods lived across the street and came barreling out of his driveway at 2 am hitting the fire hydrant I would at least KNOW it was him when I called 911. I would probably even run out to help him too. Yet this neighbor, (who *was* good enough to call for help,) did not know who was lying out there in his street.

You know that reminds me of the time this really drunk Asian lady I don't know fell through my front door, cocktail in hand, and looking up from the floor (she had not spilled a drop of her half cocktail) asked if she were in the Robinson house (name changed to protect my neighbor). They were having their annual Christmas party and she had missed it by a few doors. No, I explained, that was four doors down, but could I freshen her drink? See, now that's what neighbors do. They don't go calling the police and acting like they don't even know each other.

Point Two: Rich famous women smash out car windows to save their husbands: On Tiger's website you can read his statement that his wife "acted courageously when she saw I was hurt and in trouble." Let's review: he backed into a fire hydrant and a tree and she had to smash out the BACK window to pull him out of the car? Just how pinned in do you get when you back into a fire hydrant? How strong is this woman that she could drag an inert full grown man from the front seat and out the back window? Maybe she panicked and it was the butler's night off so she had to do it herself. And she just grabbed the first thing she saw which was a golf club which they probably have laying all over their house and yard since Tiger is a golfer.

Now if I were "acting courageously" and wanted to "help my husband out of the car" I would not grab a golf club. Why? Because my husband doesn't care about golf. I would grab one of his guitars and then I would "courageously" smash out his back window and "help" him out of the vehicle by beating him with the guitar. I'm just saying.

Point Three: Rich and famous people get to tell the police "We need some privacy" and that works: If you or I were to knock over a fire hydrant, and run into a tree, and CLEARLY were involved in the middle of a domestic disturbance, we would not get to tell the Police the following morning they should respect our privacy. Well, I guess we could say those words but I doubt they would tip their hats and say, "Sorry to bother you ma'am." In fact, since there are children in the home we would probably get a little visit from DCFS too and I don't think you get to tell them to "respect your privacy" either.

In conclusion, I guess things are different when you live in a gated community in Florida where the neighbors don't even know you.

Those people probably don't even have a block party there.

I'm glad I'm not rich and famous.

THE SUMMER OF '03

I saw him for the first time in a long time the other day. He stopped by for a few minutes. We laughed and joked and just for a moment it felt like old times. But it didn't last long. I could tell he was thinking of her; the latest in his succession of women; I even know her name—it's Martha, a good friend who lives in the neighborhood. He always has them lined up like that —one right after another. Sometimes he even juggles two or three at a time. He's very organized that way plus he has Oscar and Alberto to help him with the heavy lifting.

I'm talking about my contractor of course, what did you think I meant!

Yes, my contractor, Michael. He stopped by to look at a leak in my bathroom ceiling. He's the guy who added on two baths, a sunroom and an expanded kitchen for us in the summer of '03. We saw each other every day back then, that golden summer, huddled over grout samples, discussing the placement of outlets and waste water pipes. Those were heady days.

I remember running into my friend Carrie in the grocery store during that time. "How's the construction going?" she asked me.

"Great!" I said, "I love my contractor."

"Oh that's good," she said, "That makes such a difference."

"No, I mean, I LOVE my contractor."

She nodded knowingly. "That's very common. Like falling for your shrink or your doctor. They're the perfect man. They do anything you tell them to."

"I know!" I said, relieved that I was not the only one. "And he knows what I want."

"Totally!" she said.

Oh yes my friend, Michael knows what a woman wants. He should—he's been pleasing them for years. He knows we want lockers for the kids' stuff, double-hung closets, and a counter to fold our laundry. Those are just the little things he remembers. He knows about the big stuff too like making sure the workers are there on time every day and having them clean up after themselves.

Yes, we spent a glorious summer together as he knocked out walls and built my dream house. And then one day when an autumn wind blew through, and the counters finally arrived, he finished installing the garbage disposal, hooked his thumbs in his tool belt, cocked his head and declared the job to be done. And he walked out of my life for good. (Except for last year when he came and redid the basement.)

It was good to see him the other day but I could tell his mind wasn't on my leaky ceiling. No, it was on Martha's drywalling that was going up that day. I could see that. It's okay. I know, that's just how it goes. Right now it's all about Martha and that's how it should be.

I saw Martha at a neighborhood party Saturday. I couldn't help but ask her how it was going.

"It's great. It's like having a second husband!" she enthused. "When he comes in every morning I call out, 'Hi honey!'"

Damn her! I never thought to call him honey. Maybe if I did he'd still be here, fixing that leak in my ceiling. Adding shelves to the laundry room. Redoing the old bathroom that's causing the leak.

My only consolation is that this won't last. No, my dear Martha, when the counters go in and the garbage disposal is all hooked up he'll do the same to you that he did to me. He'll move on. Who knows where. Maybe an addition in Highland Park. Could be a teardown in Arlington Heights. But make no mistake, a man like Michael is always looking for the next job, moving forward, moving on. And then you'll be just like me and the rest of the women he's left behind—just another former client.

But take heart, you'll always have the summer of '09 —and that fabulous double-hung walk-in closet. No one can take that away from you.

PART 07: CANCER

LILLY LOOK BACK

Dear Friends and Family,
As we head off to Sanibel Island this weekend, I cannot help but remember that it was ten years ago this weekend, on March 25, 2002, that we discovered a lump on our daughter Lilly's abdomen.

After six grueling hours in the ER at Ft. Myers, we learned our 3-year-old baby girl had kidney cancer. We raced home to Chicago where she had her kidney and the tumor removed and received six months of chemo and radiation at Chicago Children's Memorial Hospital.

To express our gratitude to the hospital and our happiness that Lilly is ten years cancer-free, we would like to have a mini-fundraiser here online to benefit the Patient Emergency Fund at Children's Memorial.
During that grueling time, we were SO grateful to have a place like Children's Memorial that we could drive to easily for world-class care. Just a half hour away we were able to drive down for the day on treatment days and be in our own beds at night. And we were fortunate that our insurance paid for it all.

I cannot imagine going through what we did AND having to worry about getting to the hospital, where to stay, what to do with the other kids, and how to pay for it all. But that is just what many families face and I saw many of them. As if the pediatric oncology ward isn't sad enough, I would watch families numbly talking to the social worker about how they might get help paying for diapers or a place to stay.

One family in particular broke my heart. They had come from out of the country —having already lost one child to cancer they hoped to save another —leaving two more children at home in the care of a grandmother. I remember watching the social worker discretely hand them Target Gift cards so they could afford some basics. I have since learned that the Target cards and similar gifts come from a fund called the Patient Emergency Fund that is financed solely by donations. It is to this account I hope you will consider giving in honor of Lilly. Today Lilly is a completely healthy, lovely, sassy 13-year-old thanks to her successful treatment at Children's Memorial Hospital. If Lilly has ever made you smile, then please make a donation. Even a small amount would be appreciated. If you prefer to mail a check you can send one to the address below. Just include Lilly's name on the memo line so they know :

Ann & Robert H. Lurie Children's Hospital of Chicago Foundation
225 E. Chicago Avenue, Box 4, Chicago, IL 60611
Federal Tax ID: 36-357006

For all you have done. For all you do. We thank you from the bottom of our hearts.

Peace,

Judy and Jeff

CASSEROLES CURE CANCER

The first lasagna came the first night I got home from the hospital. Jeff and I were switching off between the hospital with Lilly and being home with the other two kids and it was my night home. The doorbell rang and it was my neighbor Bill. He looked ashen and held a lasagna in his hands. "I'm sorry to bother you but Marjorie and I wanted you to have this. You can freeze it if you need to." Behind him I could see my next door neighbor Sue looking disapproving. It was her job to keep the crowds away and manage the meals. Bill had slipped by her and she wasn't happy about it. I smiled and waved her off.

Under Sue's expert management, the meals came twice a week. There would have been more if we had wanted between the nursery school, the elementary school, and our church we were inundated. At one point, I ran into a friend in the grocery store. "I tried to get on your meal list but it's easier to sign up for the Titan swim classes," she said, referring to a popular class that you have to camp out for to get your kid into.

The truth is I had plenty of time to cook. We only went to the hospital for chemo once a week and the rest of the week looked (though it did not feel) fairly normal. I kidded Jean the social worker at Children's Memorial. "It's like people think casseroles can cure cancer,"

She laughed and then said, "People want to help. Let them." And so I did.

And it was good. These women, having made countless meals for each other as each child was born were expert at putting together a fabulous, nutritious, kid-friendly meal with a bottle of wine thrown in for mom and dad. But it was more than that, much more than that. Their meals were prayers in action; a ritualistic offering; quite simply they were love you could eat.

I've been remembering those days lately because I've been called on to make a few meals for church members. Young and old, facing illness and too much time in a hospital. I am so very grateful for the chance to make these meals. To give back just a little to the universe that fed us so well seven years ago. To deliver a prayer in a casserole dish.

I always said that science cured Lilly and prayer got us through it.

And the casseroles certainly helped.

STRANGER ANGELS

There's a new barista at my Starbucks. Well, she's new to that Starbucks but I know her from somewhere. She's in her late 40's, has black curly hair with some gray, and a heart-shaped face. She has a lilting accent I cannot identify (a little hispanic, a little Indian?) and speaks in sing-song. I know her from somewhere but I can't quite place her. She's not a mom from my kids' schools. Not the gym. Maybe she was a checker at the Dominicks.

As I'm standing there trying to remember how I know her she sees me and recognition lights up her face. "How are you?" she asks as if we are old friends. Damn. Still don't know. "How is your little one?" she asks. Ah, finally a clue. When someone says my "little one" I know they mean Lilly because as my youngest, she is the only one who ever traveled solo with me. So she must be someone I knew when I used to run errands with just Lilly which narrows the timeframe down to the two years that she was an "only child" while her brother and sister were in school but before she started school.

"Oh she's great!" I answer. "She's in fourth grade now."

She smiles happily. "Bring her in some time."

The next three times I go to Starbucks we more or less repeat this scene and yet I still cannot place her so one day, after I drop my two oldest off at school early and have some time to kill before Lilly has school I say, "Hey, come to Starbucks with me and see if you remember who this lady is. I'll buy you a hot chocolate." Reluctantly, she agrees.

As soon as we walk in and get in line I see the barista's face and my knees almost buckle. I do not know why but for some reason I feel like crying. I shake my head and swallow a lump in my throat, still not sure why this woman has this effect on me.

When it is our turn to order she smiles at Lilly and says in her delightful accent, "So sorry, no Forty-Niners today!" and BAM! it hits me and I know who she is. She is the waitress who served us every Tuesday at Walker Brothers' Pancake House that whole terrible time when Lilly was going through and then recovering from chemo. When she was bald and pale and couldn't eat a thing she could always choke down a few bites of her favorite pancakes—Forty-Niner-Flapjacks.

This lovely lady was the waitress we had every week who would say to Lilly, "The usual?" and bring the plate out with a flourish and a smile, knowing Lilly would only take a few bites and then she would have to wrap it all up to go. She always smiled when she saw us, always watched Lilly carefully, always served us like royalty.

There were a lot of angels in our lives during that time, five years ago,—friends, neighbors, family, church members, school friends. But there were more, these stranger-angels who helped us along and I don't even know their names like this barista. Once when Lilly had just lost all her hair we went out for dinner. It was a good night, we were laughing and having fun and when Jeff went to pay the bill the waiter said, "There is no bill sir, the gentleman who just left paid it for you." We have no idea who that generous person was, this stranger-angel.

I am thinking about all these angels again as I order my latte and a hot chocolate and I smile down on Lilly's head. When I look up I catch our stranger-angel smiling broadly at Lilly, still remarking about how tall she's gotten and how long her hair is and I say a little prayer for all the angels in our lives.

Merry Christmas

THAT'S DONE: PERIOD

Warning: if you don't know the difference between an ovary or a fallopian tube, or if TV commercials for feminine hygiene products make you run from the room—you should stop reading now.

So here's the deal. Tomorrow I have to have my uterus removed. It's because I have a "benign" tumor (uterine fibroid). I put the word benign in quotes because although it is true that it is not life-threatening (and I am exceedingly thankful for that) I would hardly call something that has caused two years of pain and six months of hemorrhaging "benign". But there you have it. And the only way to get rid of this sucker (it is embedded in the uterine wall, size of a golfball) is to take the whole dang uterus out.

It is really strange to think that after tomorrow I will never have a period again. Most people don't get to know this in advance—things just drift on until one day they realize they haven't had a period in a long time. Which got me thinking of a piece I wrote some time ago.

So in honor of my "procedure", I give you a recycled essay. To my uterus I say farewell, you served me well. To my little red-headed friend I say, good riddance, you were always a terrible friend.

This first appeared in The Chicago Tribune under the title of " Chronicling the strangest of relationships: Period" on April 21, 2004

I was talking to a good friend the other day and she told me that her daughter had just gotten her first period. My friend had been prepared for this momentous occasion and she got out the necessary products and helped her daughter with them. About an hour later her daughter came in the kitchen and said, "OK, Mom, can I take this off? Am I done yet?"

Oh honey, if you only knew. Her daughter is embarking on a very long relationship that lasts from puberty to menopause with her new "friend". If I were to tell her what I've learned about this relationship (which I wouldn't, there's no reason to send her screaming back to her childhood) here's what I'd say.

It will be a strange and dysfunctional relationship but it will follow a fairly predictable chronology. First, you will start out hating and loathing your new friend. No filmstrip or book or talk from mom can convince you that this is "beautiful". It's uncomfortable, painful, messy, and embarrassing. It requires the use of mysterious, unwieldy products you have never even seen let alone know how to use. With the help of a best friend shouting directions through the door you will finally figure out how to use the more challenging but effective products. Eventually, say in 5 to 10 years, you will even master said products so that you are not totally uncomfortable with your new friend. But then you will do something to mess up this relationship. You will become sexually active.

Now, instead of loathing her, you look forward to seeing your friend every month. She is a reassuring and visible sign that you have not made the biggest blunder of your life. Even if you are exceedingly careful, you will not know real relief until you see concrete evidence of her return. Cramps are not enough. You need proof of your freedom. There are times you are less cautious than others. On these occasions you will not be just glad to see her, you will fall on your knees and thank God she has returned. You will reassure her that next time you will take every precaution necessary to ensure her timely return. The relationship will continue along like this for some time.

Then one day you will hear the unmistakable ticking of your biological time clock. Now you will find yourself in an upside-down world in which you will try, very, very hard to achieve a physical state that you have tried very, very hard to avoid for a very, very long time. This will seem very, very strange.

Most of us will be in this phase for what seems like an eternity even if it is in fact only a few months. Each month you will not only hate the mere hint of your friend's return, you may actually be moved to tears of bitter disappointment at the sight of her. You will resent that the pregnancy tests are placed so closely to the sanitary products at the drugstore. The longer this phase goes on, the more you will come to hate her. Sadly, because of the vagaries of life, some women will find themselves in this phase for many years without a happy resolution. If you are fortunate enough to reproduce more or less when you want to, you will finally rejoice at your friend's absence. If she is even a day late you will run out to the drugstore and purchase your EPT kit and wave that magic wand around in glee.

For the next several months your friend will be replaced by a myriad of bodily changes that are absurdly taxing, but you will not wish for the return of your friend's relatively gentle presence. One day, quite suddenly, you will remember her for a few nostalgic moments as your labor begins. But your friend is to labor as a chimp is to King Kong and you will soon forget her again.Nursing will keep her away for a few more months and then one day, she will return and you will be happy to see her again. She will remind you that your body no longer belongs to another tiny being but is in fact returning to you.Now you will be back to the days of welcoming her every month, glad to know that at least for now your body is your own. Until you decide your child needs a sibling, then you can revert to the days of dreading the sight of her again.And so it goes. Until one day your house is full of children and you realize you are done.

But strangely, your body does not. Though you are mentally and physically past the optimal age to reproduce, your body keeps trying to. You do not want to be like someone in the Old Testament and you return to the days of fearing her presence. Even if your husband has been "fixed" you know that mistakes can happen.These days stretch into months and years and your old friend will visit with less and less regularity. Sometimes she'll stop by for a brief unexpected visit and other times she will hunker down for an extended stay. And then one day, without any word of warning, she will disappear for good. Like all old friends, you will not realize that her last visit is her last.

As my friend's daughter begins this relationship I am fast approaching the end of my relationship. I don't know how I'll feel when I realize my friend has left for good but I suppose I'll be as conflicted about her departure as I've always been about her arrival. I'll be relieved she's finally gone but no doubt a little regretful to see her leave forever.

CARINGBRIDGE AND A COOLER

Oh crap. The surgery I wrote about below did not go as expected. When they opened me up they found out the benign tumor was not. Miraculously, the gynecological oncologist who is only in the hospital once a week was there. They found her to finish the surgery. After five hours of emergency surgery and two pints of blood they sewed me back up.

It appears I have a rare form of uterine cancer. Something called Leiomyosarcoma. It means (roughly translated) "benign fibroid that decides to turn into cancer". One in a million or something.

Having gotten Lilly through this with her rare cancer eight years ago we are beyond devastated. How on earth do two people from one family have rare cancers? I eat blueberries. I do yoga. I don't use pesticides. I don't even use weed killer for God's sake. But there you have it.

I am only going to write about this once here on this blog and then I want to return to writing about other things. If you would like to follow my medical progress, you are free to do so at my Caringbridge website http://www.caringbridge.org/visit/judyzimmerman

In my neighborhood when someone is in trouble the women rally like an army with meals. The afflicted family puts a cooler at the back door which is filled on a regular basis. The cooler is there so no one has to greet the food giver and try to make small talk which can be exhausting.

No one wants to be the one with the cooler at the back door.

Jeff and I will be traveling to Boston in a week or so to see the specialists for this thing I have. I'll let you know by Caringbridge what we find out. Though they caught this early, treatment is likely as it is aggressive.

This thing is aggressive and rare. Just like me.

OKAY, ENOUGH OF THAT

As most of you know I have been struggling with a new cancer diagnosis and subsequent information from the medical establishment that seemed to be getting worse and worse by the week. This has had the understandable and normal effect of scaring the crap out of me (and my family) and making me feel very sad, even depressed despite all the wonderful support and prayers from you all.

Today it changes. I am taking back my life. I am tired of worrying about the worst that could happen. I am ready to expect only the best and then some.

I am ready to heal.

I believe in the incredible power of the human body. I believe in the power of mind over matter. I believe in the power of prayer. I believe in my own body's ability to heal. I believe in the power of being loved and cared for by a multitude of family and friends.

The only thing any of us has is today and today I feel damn good. I am strong and have no pain. I look damn good. The sun is shining and it is a gorgeous fall day.

I am ready to heal.

TO SLEEP PERCHANCE TO DREAM

One of the worst symptoms so far of this new illness I have is that it causes insomnia. Not just for me but for all my loved ones too. I don't think Jeff, my parents, my sister, or Coffee Friend 2 have had a good night's sleep in several weeks. Coffee Friend 1 does but that's because she takes Ambien. Although, even that didn't work for her those first few days after my surgery.

We compare notes and ask each other what time we woke up, trying to figure out if we should just get together every night at 3:00. Poor Coffee Friend 2—when she wakes up she never goes back to sleep—just lays there "waiting for the f***-ing sun to come up" as she said. My parents told me they wake up at 3:00 and ask the other one if he/she is asleep. My sister-in-law in LA said, "I went to sleep worrying about Judy, dreamed about her all night, and woke up thinking of her."

I myself seem to wake up at exactly 1:30 and 4:30 every night.

I am normally blessed with the ability to fall asleep and stay asleep. It's a gift really. As I have often said, I respect sleep and it respects me. But even I wake up a couple of times a night and play "what if" in my mind. I find if I talk to my Grandma Zimmerman at those times it helps. I can fall back asleep. Grandma Z. died in 1990 by the way but we still chat when I'm worried about things. She's very reassuring.

When we found out about Lilly's illness on vacation in Florida we tried to go to sleep that first night and I don't think I slept a minute. When we got up I told Jeff that was the worst night's sleep I never had. My mom said she had slept like a baby—she woke up every two hours and cried.

I hate that I am keeping people up at night. But what can you do? That's what happens when people love you.

Last night Jeff slept well for the first time since my surgery because we finally had a good day with some good news. I still found I had to have a chat with Grandma but I'm hopeful that this symptom will go away soon.

For anyone else out there who has had trouble sleeping, I apologize. I hope your insomnia is gone now, but if you still have trouble you can always talk to my Grandma about it.

DRUGS

As a yogini who pops an aspirin reluctantly it is rather jarring to find I suddenly have a counter-top full of drugs. Most of them are to fight side-effects of the most toxic drug of all—chemo—so a little bit of this and that shouldn't bother me but it takes some getting used to.

I'm learning a lot about these drugs. One is that it's pretty damn easy to mix them up. On Sunday I woke up a little nauseous and asked Jeff to bring me a Zofran (anti nausea). He did and I fell back to sleep for two hours. When I woke up and told him I was still nauseous he admitted had misunderstood and brought me a Xanax (anti-anxiety) instead (they do both start with a Z sound). Which explained why I was still nauseous but curiously not worried about it.

Last night I learned not to mix Benadryl (for the itchy rash the chemo gave me) with Xanax because it makes me jittery and have strange dreams in which I am in Los Angeles and unemployed actors are used to help street vendors sell fruit and tacos through elaborate song and dance sequences that are like a cross between *Glee* and that market scene in *Oliver*. Wait, they don't really do that do they?

And that's just a snapshot of the legal drugs. Do you know how many people tell you they can score medical marijuana for you when they learn you have this disease? My nieces and nephews I expect. Some of my hardier partying friends I expect. But my aunt and uncle? Well, they do live in California. But the funniest was the offer that came from a certain nonagenarian family member who shall remain nameless. Now that is generous.

Okay, I'm off to enjoy a dose of a slightly less toxic but legal drug — caffeine.

EDITOR'S NOTE: *As the author's condition worsened she stopped blogging for fear of depressing people and switched to medical updates for friends and family on The Caring Bridge website. Several weeks after entering hospice in suburban Chicago she passed quietly on December 26th, 2013. When she was first diagnosed doctors gave her 18 months to live. She made it three years and three months proving once again she always did things her way. Judy Zimmerman was 53.*

JUDY'S LAST WORDS

Goodbye Friends. Love and Peace To You All
Journal entry by Jeffrey Ludwig — Dec 28, 2013
Family and Friends,

Sadly, I am writing on Judy's behalf. Judy died peacefully on Thursday, December 26 around 7:30 pm. If you have been following Judy's story, you know she fought courageously for almost three and a half years. Before I share more of Judy's story with you, I want to express my deepest appreciation for the inspiring support that so many of you have provided over this time. Your encouragement, prayers, and heartfelt love as captured in your Caring Bridge entries were a constant source of power, energy and nourishment for Judy's long and difficult struggle. Your active participation in Judy's fight is evidence that love and kindness are all around us.

 At its core, it is the only reason we are here. That is what Judy came to understand and express. Sometimes I suppose we need to be reminded of that. That is one explanation for Judy's suffering and she acknowledged the importance of that peculiar relationship between love and the pain of suffering. Her inspiring example is proof that she accepted that responsibility and carried out her mission with such grace and love for us all.

In Judy's final days and hours, she found it difficult to talk and express her thoughts clearly. That is not surprising given all that she had been through. However, she smiled at the sight and sound of Atticus, Grace and Lilly; her parents Frank and Faye; her siblings Debbie, Paul, and John and her endless list of friends. She squeezed our hands when we held her. Quiet and alone with me she would repeat only a single word — love, love, love. I and my children and all who came to know Judy are blessed with her love.

Finally, allow me to express my condolences. I am so sorry for your loss.

Below is a farewell note to you all.
Jeff

Farewell From Judy

Beloved, thank you for gathering to say goodbye to me. Never an easy thing for any of us so I appreciate it. Know truly in your hearts that I am in a better place after a LOT of suffering and it was just time to move on to a better place.

I end my generous days (I would have liked another 30 years!) feeling completely fulfilled having known true, deep, great love, with Jeff, truly the love of my life as you all know. We ended each day calling each other true love and referred to each other as soul mate.

I have three children who have brought me joy every day of my life, and I beg them to move on from their grief knowing that the way they treated me earned them the right to live their own wonderful sweet, fulfilled lives that do not require them to wander around feeling badly about any of this. It is simply part of life and unfortunately a part of theirs.

As for what I have been blessed with...well it is ridiculous. I come from a loving, tight knit family. I met my soul mate at a young age. I had access to higher education and world travel and I even lived overseas where I made life-time friends I am still in contact with.

Later in life I have been blessed with a community of friends so tight it almost seems made up — most especially since moving to Glenview where everyone seems designed to take care of me and my family especially since Lilly got sick but even more since I got sick.

No words can thank you all for all you have done. Really. The meals are just the tip of the iceberg and as you know they have been non-stop since I was first diagnosed.

(Here, I am not going to mention names because I am sure to miss someone)

The prayers, cards, letters, notes (many of you have sent them weekly), prayers, tears, rides for Lilly (two friends have driven her every day this year), rides to chemo (most from just a few of you), prayers, meals, (one family has made us a meal every other week for three years AND decorated my flower pots!), prayers, coffees (always available at the drop of a text), and prayers.

As for my family...my sister has pretty much given up her life to care for me for the past three years as have my parents. And my brothers came from the west coast numerous times.

Did I mention my life has been blessed?

So go forth friends. From me I hope you have learned to love as hard as you can and celebrate every day.

Judy

AFTERWORD

Because of my mom, my family has a reason to celebrate every December 26th. This newfound celebration, an extension of the holiday season, became a part of my family's tradition so seamlessly that it seems strange to consider that there was ever a time in my family history where we didn't celebrate the 26th. This year, we celebrated with an incredible meal at Trattoria 10 in Chicago. Dinner was followed by a family viewing of Hamilton, in memory of my mom's passionate (sometimes to the point of embarrassment) affection for theatrical arts, which of course Grace and I carried on by reenacting every Schuyler sister scene on our way to the theater.

Throughout the night, we caught up with one another, at times playfully joking at each other's expense, but always returning to a thematic conversation of support, encouragement, and togetherness. My siblings made fun of me for the embarrassing photos I'd drunkenly posed for the night before, on Christmas. Atticus and I teased Grace for her inability to digest literally any of the entrées on the menu (as usual, she was forced to order a custom gluten-free and vegan meal from the chef). All of us remembered, with fondness, just how terrible of a cook my mom was. (I mean really, she was bad. If you ever had to eat a Judy Zimmerman casserole, you know what I mean.) My dad discussed the possible pronunciations for the city of Melbourne ("is it, mel-BON, or is it, mel-BURN?"), which prompted him to recall the five to ten years after my mom returned from her study abroad trip to Spain, in which she interjected in every conversation possible: "well, when I lived in Spain." When our drinks arrived, I toasted to "a beautiful life and a beautiful family."

We do this every December 26th. These evenings are always attended by myself, Atticus, Grace, and our dad. Throughout the years, new faces have joined our table. As me, my siblings, and our dad welcome new love into our lives, we've expanded our family's collective capacity for love as well. These dinners are an extension of my mom, and if you knew her, you can understand why. Like our mom, these evenings represent my family's value in laughter, celebration, love, and the intensity of the human experience. The new faces that we welcome to these nights don't fill her space, for there is no space to be filled. They simply expand the love that was present during her life — love so deep, it could never be taken away by death.

By now, you can probably tell that my family is close. We're not "oh we get together for the big holidays" or "we pose for these nice pictures" close. We actually really like each other! Us three kids have found a deep appreciation for the passions and skills of the others. We frequently call upon one another for advice and support. And our dad… our dad has shown up for us as an ideal role model of a man. He is steady. He is gentle. He is generous. He is available, emotionally and otherwise. He is genuinely interested in our lives, although they are so different than the youth that he experienced. There is nobody in this world who has my back like my dad and my siblings. And when I think about losing my mom, all I see is this beautiful family that she gave me. If I had never received anything from my mom except for my loving dad and siblings, then that would have been enough — she would have fulfilled her role as a mother.

A few weeks after our family celebration on the 26th, my mom came to me in a dream, which she does from time to time. It was the night before my "last first day" of college. In my dream, my mom was telling me how excited she is to see me graduate in May. When I woke up, my alarm was one minute away from going off. I like to think that she had gotten me up for my first day of the semester. I walked to my closet to get dressed for class, and her University of Michigan sweatshirt literally fell out of my closet onto the floor. I smiled to myself and slipped it over my head. Feeling extra connected to her, I took five minutes to meditate and reflect on our dream together. I pulled a card from Doreen Virtue's Talking to Heaven, a deck of 44 oracle cards that channel messages from loved ones who've crossed over. After shuffling the deck, I pulled a card that read: "We have been together in dreams." Afterward, I got into my car to head to campus The first song that came on my shuffle was Miley Cyrus's "Mother's Daughter." I smiled to myself, knowing that she had done everything she could to send me off to school. The whole day I felt her love, presence, and the warm hug of her Michigan sweatshirt around me.

This is only one example of the many ways that my mom stays active in our lives. I see evidence of my mom living on everywhere I go. I see her in my sister's compassion. I see her in my brother's curiosity for the world. I see her in my dad's loyalty to his family. I see her in my grandparent's commitment to one another. I see her in my aunt and uncles' dedication to laughter, joy, and fun. I even see her through the unwavering support of our family dog, my mom's closest four-legged companion, Molly.

And if this concept is difficult for you to conceptualize, then I invite you to see her existence in this book. Her book. Her words. These words came from her, and in writing them down, she left a part of herself here on earth, forever. Every time we read these words, we're giving them the power to bring her back to life. This book is proof that life is so rarely dependent on the human vessel.

Observing the ways in which my mom is still so connected to her family has taught me that Judy can be present in every aspect of our lives if we give her permission to show up and if we give ourselves permission to feel close to her.

Throughout my childhood, my mom wore two rings on her finger. One was the wedding band that represented her 29 year marriage to my dad (she passed away 4 months shy of their 30th anniversary). They were so young when they got married that they were too poor to buy an engagement ring, so for 20 years, she simply wore her wedding band. The second ring was a simple band with three diamonds, representing her three children, that my father gave to her for their 20th wedding anniversary (she got my dad a beautiful Tiffany watch). When I was probably eight or nine years old, my mom took off her rings and put them into my small palm. She pointed to her anniversary ring, the one with the diamonds.

"See how this isn't a perfect circle?" she said to me, running her index finger over the band until it stopped at the diamonds.

I nodded. Then she pointed to her wedding band, and began to move her index finger in a complete circle, her finger gently touching the rim of the band.

"Life is like this ring," she said to me. "It's a complete circle. It continues. It goes on forever. Even after death."

—Lillian Ludwig, representing the Ludwig children / February / 2020

Made in the USA
Coppell, TX
28 March 2024

30666183R00189